The Cambridge Manuals of Science and Literature

T0351980

EARLY RELIGIOUS POETRY

OF PERSIA

EARLY RELIGIOUS POETRY OF PERSIA

BY

JAMES HOPE MOULTON, M.A.

D.Lit. (Lond.), D.D. (Edin.),
D.C.L. (Durh.), D.Theol. (Berlin).
Greenwood Professor in the
University of Manchester

Cambridge :
at the University Press
1911

CAMBRIDGE UNIVERSITY PRESS
Cambridge, New York, Melbourne, Madrid, Cape Town,
Singapore, São Paulo, Delhi, Tokyo, Mexico City

Cambridge University Press
The Edinburgh Building, Cambridge CB2 8RU, UK

Published in the United States of America by Cambridge University Press, New York

www.cambridge.org
Information on this title: www.cambridge.org/9781107605794

© Cambridge University Press 1911

First published 1911
First paperback edition 2011

A catalogue record for this publication is available from the British Library

ISBN 978-1-107-60579-4 Paperback

Cambridge University Press has no responsibility for the persistence or
accuracy of URLs for external or third-party internet websites referred to in
this publication, and does not guarantee that any content on such websites is,
or will remain, accurate or appropriate.

*With the exception of the coat of arms at
the foot, the design on the title page is a
reproduction of one used by the earliest
known Cambridge printer, John Siberch, 1521*

IN PIAM MEMORIAM

EDVARDI BYLES COWELL

ΤΡΟΦΕΙΑ

PREFACE

THE fascinating field of Avestan literature has been strangely neglected in our country. I have tried in a modest way to open it up for students of poetry and students of religion, who will I trust at least recognise from these pages that the subject is worth pursuing further. The little book ventures on ground which is full of pitfalls for investigators who are not able to give undivided attention. I have therefore appreciated very specially the help of two old friends who have looked over my proofs—the Editor, with whom I read the Gâthâs under Cowell long ago, and (for the first half of the book) Prof. Williams Jackson, whose paramount authority in Iranian subjects every expert knows. To them and to other scholars named in the book itself I offer very warm thanks, only asking the reader not to hold them responsible when I have dared to be original— and very likely wrong.

J. H. M.

Wesleyan College, Didsbury.
August 1911.

CONTENTS

TRANSCRIPTION AND PRONUNCIATION

The alphabet which appears in Avestan MSS is replaced throughout with Western letters. The system of transliteration here adopted has been governed mainly by the desire for simplicity: no attempt has been made to differentiate certain sounds which have separate symbols, but no intelligible distinction of quality. Transliterations enclosed in brackets are used in the body of the text, the others where an Avestan or Old Persian word is given as such.

Vowels :—

a ā (ā in *father*)	ą (as in French *an*)
e ē (cf. u in *but*)	å (as in *law*)
ę ē̜ (as in *let*, *fête*)	i ɪ (as in qu*i*n*i*ne)
o ō (as in n*o*te)	u ū (as in p*u*ll, p*oo*l).

Consonants :—

k	w
g (hard)	ṅ (ng) (as in sa*ng*)
χ (kh) (as in lo*ch*)	n
γ (gh) (dialectic Ger. Ta*g*e)	m
c (ch) (as in *ch*ur*ch*)	y
j (as in *j*udge)	v
t (hard)	r (trilled)
d	s (as in *s*eal)
θ (th) (as in ba*th*)	z (as in *z*eal)
δ (dh) (as in ba*the*)	š (sh) (as in *s*ure)
ṭ (th) (? nearly = θ or δ)	ž (zh) (as in a*z*ure)
p	h
b	χᵛ (hv) (as in Welsh *chw*ech).
f	

CHAPTER I

THE ARYANS AND THEIR LANGUAGE

THE continent of Asia, apart from the tiny country of Palestine, has produced very little poetry that has made any impression upon the West. The vast literature of India is known at a respectful distance, and its philosophy has to some extent compelled recognition; but the genius is yet unborn who shall popularise Veda or Mahâbhârata in Europe. One Eastern country alone, beyond the fortieth parallel of longitude, has sung so as to make the West listen; and that is Persia, whose early religious poetry is the subject of this little book. We are not concerned with the times that gave us Firdausi or Háfiz, Nizámi and Omar Khayyám. The poetry of our period is utterly unknown in Europe and America except to a handful of scholars. We compare our FitzGerald's Omar with the *Rubáiyát* in sober English prose, and we are inclined to see a sufficient reason in Horace's

carent quia vate sacro. Of FitzGerald and Omar we
are tempted to ask

Which is the Potter, pray, and which the Pot?

Would Omar have been heard of in English literary
circles had (say) Carey translated him?

To answer that question is not our present busi-
ness, nor does a similar question arise in connexion
with the literature we are about to describe. There
is no FitzGerald, to begin with, and if there had been,
one must doubt whether he would have found a subject to his mind. Speaking generally, this early
Persian religious poetry interests the thinker more
than the man of letters. It has not a little beauty,
and the student of religion lets his plummet down
into its depths with increasing wonder. But there is
no modernity about it, and no mirage of antiquity to
quicken a poet's fancy. The oldest and most important parts of it are sermons in metre, and perhaps
rather dull sermons too for those who are not
seriously minded. Yet it may be hoped that before
this little book comes to its last page the modern
reader may be stirred to some interest in the
doctrine of God and Man proclaimed perhaps
thirty centuries since by the Prophet Zarathushtra
(Zoroaster), whose dim figure through the mists of
time looms large among the highest thinkers of
humanity.

At a period which in the hoary annals of Egypt or Babylonia might be counted as fairly recent, there lived together in Western Asia a people who called themselves Aryans[1]. They formed the easternmost branch of the great speech-family in which our Germanic tribes have held one of the most westerly positions since history began tardily to fling us a recognition. Linguistic science enables us to reconstruct a common language, spoken in prehistoric times by a closely linked assembly of tribes occupying central or northern Europe. We only infer this common language by the careful analysis of historical dialects that are derived from it : a Hindustani word is compared with an English, a French word with a Russian, a Welsh with an Armenian, and the linguistic changes which have carried them so far apart are recognised as we trace the history back to the earliest speech we know. The actual home of the original "Indo-Germanic" or "Indo-European" tribes we cannot determine with certainty, though "somewhere in Europe" is at present the reasoned and confident answer of science to a question which fifty years ago produced the merely instinctive but equally confident "somewhere in Asia." At the very dawn

[1] The term is generally used in England in the sense popularised by Max Müller, to denote what we call Indo-European or Indo-Germanic. In this book "Aryan" always has the narrower and more correct connotation of Indo-Iranian.

of our historical knowledge one section of the family was some distance beyond the frontier of Europe towards the south-east, and it is this section with which we are concerned.

The unity of ancestry that binds together the Indian and the Persian languages is, like the larger unity, a scientific induction and not proved from actual monuments. The oldest relics we possess of these languages reveal dialects already as distinct as Dutch and English. But the most casual acquaintance soon shows that the application of a few simple sound-changes will suffice to turn the one language into the other. For instance, we find that an *s* at the beginning of a word before a vowel becomes *h* in the Iranian languages. *Seven* is *saptá* in Sanskrit, and retains its initial *s* in all the languages derived from Sanskrit. In Iranian it is *hapta*, as in Greek. Our familiar proper name *Indus* betrays by its initial, when contrasted with the native *Sindh*, the fact that it comes to us from a foreign source : the *h* that is still preserved in *Hindu* tells us that the source is Persian. The application of this and similar laws of change will enable us to turn whole pages of the oldest Iranian into the dialect of the Rigveda, and comparatively seldom find an independent variation of form. Thus Professor Geldner cites a line of the Gâthâs which he sets by the side of one from the Mahâbhârata, thus :—

(Gâth.) kē mē nā θrātā vistō anyō [ašāṭ] θwaṭ[cā]?
(M.bh.) na nas trātā vidyatē [vai] tvad anyaḥ.

The latter is negative, and uses the finite verb instead
of the participle. Otherwise, except for two words,
they would become identical if we altered them thus
(writing the Sanskrit without "sandhi") :—

      (1) kē mōi nā θrātā vistō anyō θwaṭ ?
      (2) kas mē nā trātā vittas anyas tvat?

In the application of this process on a larger scale
we not seldom find the Iranian nearer the original
when they disagree. We can best appreciate the significance of this if we take a stanza of verse in English
and write under each word the cognate word in Dutch.
We should have to try Scotch instead before we could
reduce the differences to the level of our Aryan comparison. It has seemed worth while to present this
affinity in a form which can be appreciated without
knowledge of either language, because of the fundamental importance of the issue involved. The difference of pronunciation between such a passage as
we have printed above and the Aryan form of it, as
reconstructed by the comparative method, is no
greater than that between the English of Chaucer
and that of Tennyson. We are allowed to be content with a few centuries of separation between the
two branches, lying behind our oldest representative
literature. Then we come to the period of unity, in

which the line above quoted would run somewhat as follows, allowing for some uncertainties and a margin of small dialectic differences which we cannot detect to-day :—

    (3) kas mai nā trātā vit^stas anyas tvad ?

During this period we may picture the Aryan tribes living together in a fairly extended country perhaps round the south-west of the Caspian Sea. Their language would be homogeneous enough for mutual understanding, though we may presume dialectic differences much like those which distinguish the speech of different English counties. To their common religion we shall return later. The cleavage that ultimately scattered the Aryan tribes was very probably social in its character. Part of the population were settled on the land as agriculturists, another part were nomads. The latter behaved to the former much as the Kurds behave to the Armenians in the same regions still. But at last great hordes of nomads hived off to the south-east, seeking more productive fields for plunder ; and establishing themselves in the Panjâb they ultimately became the masters of India and the authors of its intellectual wealth.

    We are concerned here with the tribes that remained behind in Iran, as the country came to be called : it is *Airyanem Vaējō*, "the Aryan

country (?)," in the Avesta. How far their territory
extended in prehistoric times we need not enquire at
this point; but we may remind ourselves that Iranian
languages to-day may be found in Persia, Afghanistan,
Bokhara, Kurdistan, Baluchistan, and as far north-
west as the Ossetes in the Caucasus. Iran, then, is
the bridge between Europe and India ; and Iranian
languages still mark the road along which our own
kith and kin migrated from Europe ages before
history began to tell of the peoples they left behind.
Antiquity preserves for us three dialects from Iran.
The remarkable discoveries at Turfân within the last
decade have added a fourth, in the Christian and
Manichaean manuscripts in the Sogdianian dialect.
These are of the highest interest to the linguist as
well as the theologian, but do not concern us here.
Nor must we do more than mention the Old Persian
language, preserved for us upon the cliff at Behistan,
where the servants of Darius and Xerxes smoothed
the surface of the rock and cut the great cuneiform
inscriptions which through twenty-three centuries
have told of the victories of Persian kings to any
travellers who risk their necks in the climb.   But if
Alexander passed that way, it is doubtful whether his
Persian guides could have read to him the parts of
the royal annals in which Marathon and Salamis were
so unaccountably passed over.   The Old Persian
quickly lost its ancient flexions, and developed into

the Pahlavi of the Sassanian era and the almost uninflected Persian of the modern period. How Grotefend and Rawlinson recovered the key of this long-lost writing, and with it opened the door to the new science of Assyriology, is a long and fascinating story on which we may not enter—the story of one of the mightiest triumphs of human intellect. The records of the Behistan Rock are told in sober prose, or we might find excuse to linger before that wonderful relic of the past. We must be content to refer our readers to an intensely interesting book of travel by one of the greatest of Oriental scholars, *Persia Past and Present*, by Professor A. V. Williams Jackson, of Columbia University, who in 1903 climbed the Rock and read afresh some of the comparatively few characters which time had obscured to Rawlinson's penetrating eye.

We pass on to the two dialects in which are written the literature that forms the subject of this little book. They have the common name of *Avestan*, from the Avesta, the sacred library of the ancient Persian religion. The name *Zend* is often given to this language; and there really does not seem to be any very convincing reason why a short and convenient term should be discarded merely because it happens to be based on a misunderstanding of the (to most of us) unknown tongue to which it

belongs. However, as science has banned the word,
we have no choice but to obey. We proceed to
define the two varieties of Avestan. The older we
call *Gâthic*, as the dialect of the Gâthâs or Hymns,
the most ancient and by far the most important
section of the Avesta, though scanty in bulk by
comparison with the rest. The *Later Avestan* is a
dialect closely akin to the Gâthic, but manifestly
separated from it by many generations, if indeed
we may not conjecture that its immediate parent
was not the Gâthic itself but a contemporary dialect
diverging from it in a few features of pronunciation.

NOTE.—The possibility of throwing light on the prehistoric
period of Aryan unity has been raised lately by the Mitanian
inscriptions discovered at Boghaz-keui by Winckler, dated in the
fourteenth century B.C. Pending further researches by the discoverer, we must recognise results as tentative; but it seems
clear that names of Aryan divinities have been found, the form
of which antedates the phonetic change of *s* to *h* described above
(p. 4). Whether their origin is Indian, Iranian (of a pre-Gâthic
dialect), or proto-Aryan, is still debated. The *Journal of the
Royal Asiatic Society* for 1909 and 1910 contains several interesting papers on the subject.

CHAPTER II

GENERAL DESCRIPTION OF THE AVESTA

THE Avesta was brought to the West in the year 1771. Manuscripts were before that date reposing in European libraries, notably the Bodleian, but no one could read them, and the little noticed Oriental curiosity was a book with seven seals. Fairly copious notices of ancient Persian religion, and even allusions to the Avesta, existed in classical authors; and they had been collected and examined with great wealth of learning by the Oxford scholar, Thomas Hyde, in a massive work published in 1700[1]. But the Parsi Dasturs of Bombay kept their secret to themselves until it was tempted from them by the Frenchman Anquetil du Perron. He had seen an Avestan manuscript and conceived the ambition to interpret it to the Western world. He reached Bombay in the face of manifold difficulties, gained the confidence of the

[1] *Historia Religionis veterum Persarum eorumque Magorum* (Oxford).

Parsis by his enthusiasm, and after many years of
study brought his treasures to Europe for publication. Anquetil's translation is of course entirely
superseded now, for reasons that will shortly appear,
though his collection of traditions is still serviceable.
But it need hardly be said that this does not detract
from the glory due to the great pioneer. It is sad to
have to record that the discoverer's reward came
mostly long after he had passed beyond the enjoy-
ment of it. A chorus of scepticism assailed him. A
leader in it was Sir William Jones, the very man who
ought to have been foremost in recognising Anquetil's
merit and correlating his discovery with the newly-
found treasures of Sanskrit. Jones was himself a
pioneer in Sanskrit study, and well acquainted
with Persian. It is strange that the acute scholar
who first saw the linguistic connexion of Sanskrit,
Greek, Latin, and Germanic, and thus laid the
foundation of all modern philology, could not see
how the new Avestan dialect, obscured though it
was by imperfect traditional interpretation, fitted
in with the facts he already knew.

The Avestan manuscripts which were thus brought
within the range of Western scholarship are all of
quite recent date: the oldest known is dated
1278 A.D. They are written in a script of relatively
late origin, running from right to left, in an
alphabet of great richness, comprising some fifty

different signs. It has retained the Aryan sibilants, and developed a number of fresh spirants (sounds like *f, v, th,* etc.), giving the language some of the characteristic softness of Spanish or Modern Greek; while it resembles all the Indo-European languages in dropping the difficult "voiced aspirates" (*bh, dh, gh*), which only Sanskrit and its descendants have kept. It has considerably augmented the scanty vowel-system it inherited from the Aryan period, in which primitive *a, e* and *o* were already fused together.

The divisions of the Avesta must here be noticed. First in importance comes the *Yasna* ("worship"), the kernel of which are the Five Gâthâs, already alluded to : the rest of the Yasna contains texts relating to ritual, some of them essentially similar in character to the *Yashts* (Av. *Yęšti,* "praise"—from same root as *yasna,* and nearly the same in meaning). The Yashts are hymns of praise, twenty-one in number, addressed to the *Yazatas* or "angels," of whom we shall have to speak presently. The Yasna and the Yashts include very nearly all the verse that the Avesta contains; and we may pass over the minor texts, only further naming the *Vendîdâd* (Av. *vîdaęva dâta,* "anti-demoniac law"), which is nearly all in prose, comprising the ceremonial code, with some more interesting matter to which we shall recur. Mention of other parts may be omitted, as they contain practically no verse.

The Avesta has had a long and chequered history, which has witnessed the irretrievable loss of its larger portions and an unknown amount of damage to the text of what has survived. Pliny tells us of two million verses composed by Zoroaster; and the Arab historian Tabari says that his writings were inscribed on twelve thousand cowhides. Parsi tradition accuses Alexander of destroying one of two complete copies of the Avesta in the sack of Persepolis; and the other copy at Samarkand, it is implied, vanished similarly. How far there still survived scattered copies of certain texts, and how far tradition preserved others, we have no means of knowing. To King Valkhash, who probably lived in the first century of our era, is ascribed the initiation of the work which ultimately produced our Avesta. It was taken up with great enthusiasm by the earliest monarchs of the Sassanian dynasty (226 A.D. to the Mohammedan conquest). The final revision of the text took place in the fourth century, when the canon was authoritatively settled. We have in the early Pahlavi writers descriptions of the contents of this canon, showing how much was even then believed to have been past recovery. But heavier losses still have followed. Alexander's destructiveness, if not purely mythical, was accidental: he was the last man to burn a literature of set purpose. It was otherwise with the Moslem invasion of the seventh century. When

the choice was between death with the Avesta and
life with the Koran, the palpable inferiority of the
latter was easily overlooked. The faithful remnant
who in the next century took refuge on the hospitable
shores of India, to find there a liberty of conscience
which Mohammedan Persia denied them, brought
with them only fragments of the literature that
Sassanian piety had so laboriously gathered. Altogether, Prof. Williams Jackson calculates, about
two-thirds of the Avesta have disappeared since the
last Zoroastrian monarch sat on the Persian throne.

It is not surprising that a book which has passed
through so many vicissitudes should have prompted
some questioning among critics of to-day. James
Darmesteter, one of the very greatest Orientalists
of the nineteenth century, carried scepticism to its
utmost conceivable length in his attempt to demon-
strate that the Gâthâs are no older than the first
century of our era, and that the Sassanian editors
are to be credited with very much more originality
than tradition allows them. Darmesteter's theory
was set forth in the introduction to his monumental French translation of the Avesta, published
in the *Annales du Musée Guimet* only a year before
the great scholar died, still in the forties, but with
achievement behind him large enough to give distinction to any lifetime. The theory needs prominent
mention here, because it is expounded for English

readers in the second edition of Darmesteter's translation of the Vendîdâd in *Sacred Books of the
East*. Its appearance in the standard volume from
which ordinary readers naturally get what ideas they
have of the Avesta makes it necessary to explain that
its brilliant author never made a convert among experts: we may feel quite confident that, had he lived,
he would have abandoned it himself under stress of
unbroken opposition from everyone whose opinion
was based on knowledge. The reasons for our trust
in the antiquity of the Gâthâs will come out as we
proceed. There is the subtle evidence of versification
and dialect, which would have been alike impossible
to fashion in the period to which Darmesteter assigns
them. There is the evidence of their contents, psycho-
logically incongruous if regarded as built up around
an imaginary character. The preservation of venerated
poetry for centuries by unaided tradition seems to us
very wonderful, but it is no unparalleled marvel. The
days are long past when the Homeric poems were
assumed to be late because it could be shown that
they were not written down in the age when they
were first composed. As for the rest of the Avesta,
its close connexion with religion accounts in the end
for its preservation. We know the forces which
carried our own sacred books through even hotter
fires of persecution than those which raged round
the Parsis when Islam came. Carried largely in the

memory, or furtively copied by unskilful hands, the
Gospels suffered not a little from textual corruption,
which could not be wholly repaired when in quieter
days students began to edit the sacred text from two
or three early recensions ; and in particular there
was considerable disturbance of the grammar and
orthography of the originals. But no one imagines
that the text as a whole is discredited by its having
passed through conditions which would have destroyed
mere literature, however full of genius, and however
beloved by aesthetic devotees of art. Much the same
in its own degree may be said of the Avestan texts.
Their grammar and their verse-form, except in the
constantly chanted Gâthâs (see p. 26), were badly
corrupted by their custodians through imperfect
knowledge of a sacred tongue long dead. But we
can feel little surprise at the preservation of
documents so fundamental to religion, by those
Pilgrim Fathers of Zoroastrianism who gave up
everything for their faith. And happily modern
science can apply stringent tests to assure us that
it was not cunningly devised fables they guarded
so long and so well.

CHAPTER III

AVESTAN VERSE-FORMS

FEW subjects are more overladen with technicality, and more obstinate when one would rouse the interest of the general reader, than that of Metre, especially as developed by modern scientific study. The present writer cannot hope to succeed where even specialists seem bound to fail ; but the subject cannot be altogether passed over, and we must attempt to give some general account of the elements which constitute verse in the Avesta. These are "elements" indeed in more senses than one ; for nothing more elementary can be found among all the verse-forms of Indo-European languages. Verse in the Avesta depends only on the numbering of syllables and the placing of the caesura. In his very important monograph on the *Metre of the Later Avesta*, Prof. Geldner has noted the total absence, after prolonged and various tests, of any discoverable rhythm or any certain influence by accent or quantity. There is one possible exception, if Geldner's suspicion is justifiable that three main accents as a rule may be found in the eight-syllabled verse. There may be added Bartholomae's argument to prove that in Gâthic verse enclitic pronouns and particles were normally placed after the first main accent in a verse unit. This marks the extent to which modern research has been able to trace the rudiments of any advance beyond a prosody dependent on syllable-counting alone.

The most conspicuous feature of Avestan metric system is the complete severance between the Gâthâs and the Later Avesta. In the former we have elaborate metres, differing widely in the several groups. We need not describe them here, for we must try to give some idea of them in Chap. VIII. as we come to each Gâthâ. The metre of the Later Avesta is very much simpler, and practically uniform. It consists of eight-syllable verses, very rarely (it would seem) lengthened into twelve. The only variety is in the length of the stanza, which may contain three, four or five lines. We come as near to it as English can in the metre of *Hiawatha*, which will be used for our renderings in Chap. IX. But we must remember to eliminate our accent, and be prepared as preliminary discipline to sing a quatrain of Longfellow to the Old Hundredth, by way of ridding

ourselves effectively of the element which is so vital
in English verse.

The Later Avesta is characterised by perpetual
mixture of verse and prose. According to Geldner,
there is only one section (the Hôm Yasht, *Ys.* 9)
which is wholly in verse; and we have the two
elements mingled in varying proportions till we
come to the Vendîdâd, where there is hardly any
continuous verse. We may generally assume that
the prose represents accretions of an age which
had probably lost touch with the ancient metre.
Theoretically the mixture might be ancient. Thus,
in his *Reallexikon der indogermanischen Alter-
tumskunde* (p. 134), Prof. Schrader mentions "a
combination of prose and strophically arranged verse,
to be found in the Veda as in the Edda." There is
seldom any temptation to fall back on this possibility
in the Avesta: the specimens we give in Chap. IX. will
enable the reader to judge very fairly for himself.
The metrical sequence may often have been lost by
textual corruption where the matter is old. More
often, we must believe, new matter has been added
in an age which had forgotten how to sing the old
songs, just as it had forgotten the idiom of the old
language.

There is a possible exception to break the
monotony of octosyllabic verse in the Later Avesta.
Geldner in his *Metrik* (1877) gave some specimens of

ten-syllabled lines, scattered about in the midst of
ordinary verse, without any obvious reason, to say
nothing of rhyme.   More hopeful decidedly is a
strophe which, as he says, "answers completely to
the Indian *akṣarapaṅkti* of 4 × 10 or rather 8 × 5
syllables."   It is worth quoting in the original for
some features which are discernible even by readers
who know nothing of the language.

> Yaṭ yayō dayāṭ, āaṭ daēva χᵛīsen ;
> Yaṭ sīðuš dayāṭ, āaṭ daēva tusen ;
> Yaṭ pištrō dayāṭ, āaṭ daēva ᵘruθen ;
> Yaṭ gundō dayāṭ, āat daēva pᵉrᵉðen.   (*Vend.* 3³².)

There follows a line of prose, which we cannot turn
into verse without drastic revision, and then there
are three lines of octosyllabic metre.   Prof. Cowell
rendered the whole passage thus, verse and prose
together, for his Cambridge pupils :

> At the sight of the barley the demons sweat ;
> At the sight of the fan the demons cough ;
> At the sight of the millstone the demons greet ;
> At the sight of the doughcake the demons are off.
> The demons he sends in haste away :
> From the house of the doughcake scared they fly.
> They scorch their jaws, they cannot stay,
> Where the barley storeheaps multiply.

The version of this " Pittacus Song," as Cowell called
it, will indicate the general character of a snatch of
popular poetry which breathes the whole spirit of the

early Mazdayasnian community in its enthusiasm for
agriculture. But Geldner, in his great critical edition
of the Avesta, prints these decasyllabics as prose;
and to judge from his silence on the subject in the
Grundriss (II. 23) he has given up his former view.
Prof. E. V. Arnold in a letter to the writer says, " It
seems rather doubtful whether these lines are verse:
they suggest to me rather the parallelism of form
and meaning which is the foundation of verse and
a stepping-stone towards it."

It remains for us to bring these characteristics of
Avestan verse into comparison with what we find in
India. We have already remarked on the closeness
of the nexus between the two divisions of the Aryan
language-unity; and we shall find under this new
heading some features of close relationship that are
both suggestive and perplexing. We start with
observing how the intense individuality of the Gâthâs
is maintained even in their prosody. In dialect, as
we have seen, they stand much nearer than the Later
Avesta to the Rigveda; but in metre and in thought
alike it is the Yashts and not the Gâthâs in which
the Vedic student finds himself at home. Four out of
the five verse-systems of the Gâthâs have no complete
parallel in the Veda, according to Geldner; though
Prof. Arnold in his *Vedic Metre* enumerates not less
than 88 metrical forms. We are not surprised to
find that Vedic bards developed their own metres

to a considerable extent, as lyric poets will in every age which has not fallen into slavish artificiality. That so original a thinker as Zarathushtra should have done the same need cause no surprise.

What is remarkable, and not readily explained by mere coincidence, is the fact that in metrical form the approximation between Indian and Iranian becomes most marked in the later stages of both literatures. The octosyllabic verse of the Later Avesta is found in the Veda, and provides ultimately the *çloka* of the Epic, to be numbered there by the hundred thousand. We have therefore the curious fact that later Indian and later Avestan poetry alike not only developed the same metre but practically discarded all others. Prof. Arnold is even disposed to think that the bards travelled from Persia to India : so hard does it seem to him to explain by parallel development. Contacts between India and the Persia of the Later Avestan period are distinctly suggested by some phenomena in the religion of that period ; but so far as they go the suggestions are rather of influence travelling in the other direction.

There is one detailed result of Prof. Arnold's brilliant and laborious researches which may be con-jectured to possess significance for our subject. He has shown that in the Vedic period there are a great many originally short final vowels which have become regularly long, while in classical Sanskrit they are

short again. Now we find in our MS. tradition of
the Gâthâs that all final vowels are long, whatever
their etymological record. Prof. Arnold himself
thinks that in both cases we have to do not with
a dialectical peculiarity but a metrical fashion, "due
to an artificial emphasis on final syllables partly
based on analogy, and developed by the Avestan
poets into a rule." This explanation does not seem
available for the Old Persian of the Inscriptions,
where final long vowels equally unoriginal occur in a
considerable number. One can hardly help regarding
the coincidence in this matter between Vedic, Old
Persian and Gâthic as due to a real common tendency, which Gâthic has pushed further than the
others. In that case classical Sanskrit lies outside
the area affected by this tendency ; and we recall
the fact that there are many inflexional forms in
which Gâthic and Vedic agree, while later Sanskrit
diverges, inasmuch as Vedic is not the parent of
Sanskrit, but, so to speak, its aunt. The same is
probably true of Gâthic and Later Avestan, though
this phenomenon cannot be adduced in evidence, for
in Later Avestan all final vowels (except in mono-
syllables) are impartially short : it may therefore go
back to an ancestry agreeing with Gâthic here, or to
one which is like classical Sanskrit free from this
peculiar infection.

But this is obviously uncertain ground to tread

upon, and we must pass to a less problematical result
of the comparison between Veda and Avesta. We have
noted that from first to last Avestan verse shows
no sign of dependence on quantity. Long and short
syllables are entirely indifferent, and the student of
prosody has only to count and not to weigh. Now
the verse of the Veda has manifestly passed into a
new and more developed stage, in which (as Prof.
Arnold puts it) " preferences arise for long and short
syllables, and for groups of these, at certain points in
the verse." Nor is this the only mark of development
on the Indian side. The rules of vowel-combination
which in the Rigveda (according to Whitney) cause a
vowel-ending to coalesce with a vowel initial in the
next word about seven times for every one in which
hiatus is left, mark a great change from the conditions found in the Avesta, where this "sandhi" is
relatively rare. This all means that the Rigveda
belongs to a very much more advanced stage of
literary evolution than any part of the Avesta,
although the latest Avestan poetry must be centuries later in date than the latest hymns of the
Rigveda. Indian literary development was clearly
a hothouse plant. The Vedic poets belonged to a
regular craft, like Pindar; and the bardic families
had no doubt been elaborating the lines of their
models for generations before our oldest extant hymn
was composed. In Persia, on the other hand, it was

well-nigh two thousand years before poets arose who
cared much for literary form. We may not therefore
argue that the more primitive system of Gâthic verse
gives the Hymns of Zarathushtra higher antiquity
than the oldest Indian poetry with its abundant
marks of literary development. But when we set
this mark of primitive simplicity by the side of the
evidence from language, which makes us recognise
Gâthic to lie at least as near as Vedic to the parent
Aryan, we feel it increasingly difficult to acquiesce in
the traditional date for the Prophet (p. 48 f.) if the
Vedic poets are not to be brought down out of the
second millennium B.C.

Lastly we must comment on the welcome evidence
afforded by the test of metre as to the remarkable
faithfulness with which the Gâthâs have been preserved. Our oldest MSS. were written less than six
centuries ago, and during by far the largest proportion of their long history the Hymns have been
chanted in a dead language. In spite of this they
present to modern scholarship a text which will
stand close testing by laws of metre established out
of a cognate literature of which the authors never
heard. We may as well add the transmitters also,
for even if the Parsi priests who wrote our MSS.
knew the Veda well—a sufficiently unlikely hypothesis—they could never have detected the subtle
traces of identity beneath a diversity which they

never attempted to impair. They must have done much more if they attempted anything at all. The accuracy of transmission of course arises from the unique sanctity with which the Hymns were invested, as it does in the parallel case of the *Saṃhitā* text of the Rigveda. In both Gâthâs and Veda the metre enables us to restore, on curiously similar lines, a more archaic pronunciation than our traditional spelling witnesses. We may safely assume that fixed tunes or chants preserved the metre, and so preserved the grammatical accuracy of texts in a dialect long dead. However this may be, we have beyond question copies made in the fourteenth century of our era presenting us with poems that we may compare word after word with ancient or modern speech-material from all the languages of our Indo-European family. And such comparison equally beyond all question gives us trustworthy scientific results, even though we have to believe that when the Magi chanted the Gâthâs to the rising sun as they journeyed to Bethlehem long ages ago, the language of their hymn may have been less clear to them than it is to their modern successors in Bombay.

What has been said of the Gâthâs is much less true of the Later Avesta, though (as we have seen) ritual use preserved even there a large amount of verse when the secret of its scansion and composition was lost. Priests and theologians and lovers of national folklore could add their glosses to these less venerated poems without hindrance, and the glosses might often extend beyond the bulk of the original. These glosses betray themselves to us not only by their unmetrical form, but often by grammatical blunders showing under what impossible limitations their authors tried to compose in a sacred language which for generations had never been spoken.

CHAPTER IV

EARLY HISTORY OF THE RELIGION

IN the "Religious Poetry" that forms our subject we very soon discover that the adjective bulks much larger than the noun. The merely literary side of our survey will give us but little to do. A lover of the Avesta is loth to admit it, but the confession must be made that the man whose interest in religion is only aesthetic is not very likely to tarry long in this field. It might even be suggested that one reason for the failure of Parsism to win a commanding place among the world's religions lies in its weakness on that side where literature makes itself, even when its creators, like the writers of the New Testament, are totally unconscious of any literary gift or mission. Around the figure of the Founder himself there is no halo, nor anything out of which a halo could be developed. Few facts are recorded about his life, and in his own poems he contrives to suppress his personality more than any other religious genius known to history.   Later legend about him is hardly ever picturesque.   It revels in the marvellous, but the marvels are mostly trivial or absurd.   We can admire Zarathushtra, and we can set him with thankfulness among the Prophets through whom God spake to the fathers of old time.   But we can neither realise nor idealise him : like his own angelic abstractions around the throne of his very impersonal God, he is "a voice and nothing more."

In delineating the nature of Zarathushtra's work we have to keep in mind constantly our dependence on conjecture, and we must proportionately shun any tendency to dogmatism.   It is obviously essential, in estimating the life-work of a religious reformer, that we should have a thorough understanding of the religious conditions of his own upbringing and of the people to whom he preached.   But in the case of Zarathushtra this *milieu* cannot be described from documentary evidence or recalled by ordinary historical methods.   It has to be sought in a prehistoric twilight and reconstructed by methods which are thoroughly scientific but admittedly not infallible. The nature of these methods we have sketched already : we have now to indicate some results of their application to Aryan religion.   Our reconstruction can of course only give us a partial idea of the religion of the Aryan tribes themselves, as evidenced by common elements traceable in Indian and Iranian worship. "Partial," we say, for there may well have been many features in proto-Aryan religion which died out in one branch or the other of the divided Aryan family, and therefore cannot be recognised as primitive by the only test we can apply. And it must also be remembered that common elements may be susceptible of another inter-pretation. There are two or three divine names in the Avesta which were most probably borrowed at a late period from Indian religion by way of direct polemic—Indian gods being turned into Avestan fiends[1]. Then there is a further gap in our evidence, in our having hardly any means of depicting the religion of tribes among whom these Aryans lived. As the Aryans were certainly only a dominant minority in the population, this aboriginal religion is likely to have influenced that of their overlords in many directions, just as the Dravidian cults of India influenced most profoundly the whole religious system of the Aryan castes in after days. The immensely important question of Babylonian influence has to be examined under this heading. But we may safely put this aside for the early period with which we are concerned : there does not seem to be any recog-nisable evidence for it till a much later stage in the

[1] Just as an Avestan reference to "Gaotema" is best taken as a definite attack upon Gautama the Buddha : see below, p. 141.

history of Parsism, with one exception to be mentioned presently.

There are quite enough positive traits, however,
which we can assign with certainty to the religion of
the Aryan period. To determine them we seek for
elements common to Veda and Avesta, and have only
to check our collection by eliminating what appears
to arise from later contacts. Confidence in the
resultant picture is heightened by its remarkable
agreement with the obviously truthful description of
Herodotus (I. 131 ff.) of Persian religion in the fifth
century B.C. We naturally expect to find in the
Aryan period the main lines of the religion which
the comparative method enables us to trace for
the primitive Indo-European age. In his masterly
article—or rather treatise—on "Aryan [i.e. Indo-
European] Religion" in Hastings' *Encyclopaedia of
Religion and Ethics*, Professor Otto Schrader gives
us the latest results of scientific research in a form
both novel and convincing. He makes large use of
the evidence we have of Lithuanian religion in
the period immediately preceding the advent of
Christianity. These people having remained from
prehistoric times within the district from which the
Indo-European tribes originally radiated—according
to the most probable view—preserved with least
change to a very late date the conditions pre-
vailing among the primitive folk, as linguistic and

archaeological evidence enables us to reconstruct
them[1]. (An illustration of this principle appears in the
point just noted, that the Persians, who remained in
the old Aryan country, preserved far more perfectly
than the Indians the characteristics of Aryan religion.)
Schrader adopts and reinforces the doctrine of
Hermann Usener as to "special gods" (*Sondergötter*),
presiding over particular actions or functions:
Roman religion preserves this extremely ancient
type unchanged to the last. Side by side with these
"special gods" there are the "heavenly ones"
(*deiwōs*), the great elemental forces of nature which
most seriously influence the well-being of men.
These nature-powers were not distinguished in title
from the material objects in which they resided.
Our earliest evidence presents us with "nameless
gods," that is gods worshipped without changing into
a proper noun the common noun that described their
function. A modern minor poet can personify at
pleasure by the easy resource of capitals, which was
denied to the ancients; but the difference between
"dawn" and "Dawn," "sky" and "Sky," is much the
same in one case as in the other. This is the reason
why the reconstructed language of the original Indo-
Europeans contains no real divine names. Father

[1] Schrader's own words may be cited: "Of all the Aryans [Indo-
Europeans] the Slavs are the race that remained nearest the original
home, and are thus the last to enter into history."

Heaven and Mother Earth were most assuredly worshipped, but whereas *dyēus* remained in most of the Indo-European dialects the name for the sky, it happens that no universal name survived for the earth ; and we get the erroneous impression that the cult of the common ancestor of the Vedic Dyaush-pitar, the Greek Father Zeus, the Latin Diespiter (Jupiter), the Germanic Tiu (*Tues*day), was more important than that of his consort Mother Earth, whose name varies. We might as well argue that our Indo-European forefathers had feet (πούς, *pes*, *foot*, Skt. *pād*, etc.) but no hands, since a common name for the latter does not happen to survive. Side by side with the "heavenly ones," we have the equally important, perhaps more important, cult of the dead. Two distinct strands may be observed in Greek religion, the coexistence of which in the faith of one people will help us to understand what we find among the Aryans and other branches of our family. The Olympians as a whole belong clearly to the *deiwōs*, in so far as they have taken the general character of their chief Zeus, the Sky. But the worship of the Heroes, the ancestors, appears to have touched much deeper springs in the Greek mind ; and it is significant that their general name for God comes from this side. For θεός (*dhwesós*, cf. Lat. *festus*, and especially *feralis*, "ghostly") meant originally a ghost: θεοὶ πατρῳοί, "ancestral spirits," is a phrase that retains

the most ancient meaning of the word. Roman
religion keeps the two elements even more obviously
in view, though the Latin general word *deus* or *divos*
is the old name of the " heavenly ones." It is one of
the Roman festivals of the dead which is responsible
for the still surviving superstition about marriages in
May. Now in Aryan language there were two general
words for a god, *asura* (Skt. *asura*, Av. *ahura*) and
daiva (Skt. *deva*, Av. *daēva*). The latter is of course
the Indo-European *deiwo-*, " heavenly," whose plural
deiwōs we have already referred to. The former is
an Aryan derivative from the Indo-European *ásu-*,
the breath of life, whence in the West we have Anglo-
Saxon *ése*, " elves," that is " spirits." That in Avestan
ahura came to mean " Lord," and *daēva*, " demon,"
is a fundamental part of the later history of Iranian
religion, which we must treat in its place. Here it
is enough to note that the names are significant of
the two most prominent elements in Aryan ideas
about God. Their coexistence may possibly be due
ultimately to race-mixture, the fusion of a race
worshipping ancestors with another race worshipping
the " heavenly ones." But it is not easy to find any
Indo-European folk that in primitive times worshipped
either the one or the other exclusively ; and we may
as well acquiesce in the recognition of the combination as far back as our knowledge will carry us.

Aryan ancestor-worship is represented in the

Veda by the cult of the *Pitáras*, "fathers," and in
the Avesta by the conception of the "*Fravashis* of
the Righteous," so far as they answer to the Roman
Di Manes: another side of this important conception
we shall examine below (p. 145). It will be useful
here to recall Schrader's acute remark that the
ancestor spirits rather than the *deiwōs* were the
guardians of morality. The "heavenly ones" were
the *Sondergötter* of spheres far less concerned with
human action than were the spirits of men's ancestors
that always hovered within range. An exception to
this principle might well be found in the "All-seeing
Sun" of Greek thought, which was certainly not
foreign to Indian or Iranian theology. Mithra
(below, p. 37), who is sufficiently solar to give his
name to the Sun in modern Persian (*Mihr*), is in the
Avesta the guardian of Truth (cf. p. 137 below); and
in a striking passage of the Mahâbhârata, one in
which Indian thought comes nearest to the conception of Conscience, a kingly wrongdoer is reminded
that the Sun sees secret sin. But it is hardly likely
that the idea dates from Aryan times.

The Aryan nature-gods may fairly be catalogued
in the words of Herodotus, who says that the Persians
"worshipped sun, moon, earth, fire, water and winds"
(I. 131). These answer excellently to the kind of
deities whose common recognition in Veda and
Avesta assures us that they belonged to the Aryan

pantheon. The account the same authority gives (IV. 59) of Scythian religion may be thrown into the same scale, for the Scyths seem to have been Iranians left behind in the great south-easterly migration, who preserved the Aryan inheritance in a very primitive form. He says they venerated the Hearth-fire (Hestia) most of all, and in addition Zeus and Earth. That the primeval Sky-god (Aryan *Dyauš*) still kept in the Aryan period his ancient primacy is made somewhat doubtful by the disappearance of the name from the Avesta (except in one place—see p. 124 below), and the very secondary position he takes in the Veda. But Herodotus says the Persians "called the whole orb of heaven Zeus" and worshipped him. This probably means that the historian had heard the old name, which he identified with the Greek Zeus—quite correctly, as we know. He was describing the religion of the common people inhabiting Medo-Persia, who appear to have retained in the fifth century with little change the religion their Aryan forefathers had professed in the same land at least fifteen hundred years before. The Aryans presumably worshipped Mother Earth mostly without making a proper noun out of her name ; but they seem to have created one special appellation for the Earth spirit, Aramati, which we shall find occupying a very prominent position in the Gâthâs and after (pp. 62 f.). An extremely important Aryan god whose province came

very near that of Dyauš was Mithra (Skt. *Mitra*,
Av. *Miθra* etc.). He seems to have belonged to
the upper air rather than to the sun. Prof. E. V.
Arnold says there is little support in the Veda for
the solar connexion, unless it be in hymns which
compare Agni to Mitra. Nor is the Avestan *yazata*
decisively sun-like. His name has no very convincing
cognates in Indo-European languages, and we are
rather tempted to speculate on a prehistoric link
between the Aryans and Babylon, or some source
influenced by Babylon. The "firmament" of the
first chapter of Genesis was very prominent in early
Semitic mythology ; and it is remarkable that the
Assyrian *meṭru,* "rain," comes so near to Mithra's
name[1]. If this is his origin, we get a reasonable
basis for the Avestan use of the word to denote a
contract, as also for the fact that the deity is in the
Avesta patron of Truth, and in the Veda of Friend-
ship. He is "the Mediator" between heaven and
earth, as the firmament was by its position, both in
nature and in mythology : an easy corollary is his
function of regulating the relations of man and man.
Our suspicions of Mithra's alien origin prompt the
mention here of a water-spirit who does not belong
to the Indians at all and therefore is presumably non-
Aryan. Anâhita, "the undefiled," is a river-genius,
who in the Later Avesta has a special association

[1] I owe this to my colleague Prof. H. W. Hogg. See further p. 47 below.

with Mithra, seen also in the latest of the Achae-
menian Inscriptions, and in Herodotus (I. 131), who
actually confuses the two. The name is a cult
epithet attached to a mythical river Ardvi, but the
epithet drove out the name. When however we find
that the Elamites had a corresponding deity Nahunti
(Jensen), we begin to suspect that Anâhita is an
aboriginal figure and her name among the Iranians a
product of popular etymology on familiar lines. The
very association of god and goddess which we find
here is enough to make us look towards the native cults
of Western Asia : whether Elamite or Assyrian was responsible in this case we will not presume to decide.

Next to Heaven and Earth we may take Fire,
who among the Aryans generally, as among the
Iranian Scythae (above, p. 36), held at least an
equal position to theirs, if not one higher still.
E. Lehmann acutely points out the significance of
the change which the Indian tribes made in their
conception of the sacred Fire. They used a different
word, Agni (cognate with Latin *ignis,* cf. Lithuanian
ugnìs szwentà, "holy fire"), and his special function
was the consuming of the sacrifice, which he bore up
to the "heavenly ones." But in Aryan days, as still
in the days of Herodotus (I. 132) and in the Avesta,
the sacrifice was not burnt at all, but the gods were
invited to come down and partake on the spot. Fire
then in its sacrificial aspect was the messenger that

called them down. The sacred Fire was called Âtar,
with which name we compare the Latin *âtrium*, the
room that contained the hearthfire. The Indians in
their torrid climate had no use for the old institution
which Greeks (Ἑστία) and Romans (*Vesta*) and other
northern tribes continued to regard as divine. It is
suggestive to compare the change of the old word
tepos, which connoted grateful warmth in Italy, and
gave the Scyths in their inhospitable country a
goddess Tabiti : in India it meant "penance," the
religious character of which applies in a very different
way the primitive association. Lehmann shows how
âtar was the purifier, who exorcised evil things—
illuminated the night, kept off bitter cold and wild
beasts, and destroyed noxious and devilish powers
generally. The old nomadic life on the plains might
well raise Fire to the first place among the friends
of man. The myth of the victory of Âtar over the
serpent Azhi Dahâka is thoroughly Iranian, but
it seems to go back to Aryan and even Indo-
European antiquity : Lehmann's comparison with the
saga of Loki's binding by Thor, or that of the Wolf
Fenris, is very suggestive. So is his note on the contrast of the Iranian with the characteristic Indian
myth of Indra Vṛtrahan. But he seems to be wrong
when he assumes that the primitive meaning of the
Aryan word *vṛtraghan-* was lost in Iran, as in the
Avestan Verethraghna, the genius of "Victory." On

the contrary, this is the original meaning of the word[1], which is derived from an adjective = "assault-repelling, victorious." The drought demon Vṛtra, slain by the hero Indra, is a creation of imaginative etymology : if *vṛtrahan* means "striking or slaying x," and x is an unknown quantity, the way is clear for inventing a demon with which to solve the equation. It is of a piece with the invention of a particular hell called *put* from which the *putra* (Skt. for "son") delivers his father. It would be unreasonable to expect comparative philology too early in human history !

Having thus parenthetically disposed of a further element in the Aryan heritage, we may go on to note the suggestiveness of these conceptions of a perpetual strife between powers of light and darkness, heat and cold, beneficent and malignant forces of nature. In the Aryan and early Iranian periods alike they remained purely naturalistic, and they had nothing in them to separate them in character from myths of the same order to be found in other parts of the world. But they were a very prominent feature in the mental furniture of the people to whom Zarathushtra came ; and they supplied a ready

[1] See Bartholomae, *Wörterbuch*, s.v. *vereθra* = "Angriff." Prof. E. V. Arnold remarks, "Indra appears to have stolen his title of Vṛtraghna from some earlier god or gods." It doubtless meant only "victorious" when he took it.

background for the most fundamental novelty of his
teaching, as we shall presently see. The persistence
of the naturalistic conception among the people long
after the Reformation is well seen in the myth of
Tishtrya and Apaosha, which forms the subject of
Yasht 8 (p. 132).

We need not go exhaustively through the religious
and mythological conceptions which approve themselves as primitive.   There is only one other of
primary importance, and the rest may be left till we
meet them again in the Yashts. The Aryan *Sauma*
(Ved. *Soma*, Av. *Haoma*) was originally the drink
which confers immortality, a parallel to which may
be found elsewhere in Indo-European mythology.
Such it remains in the Avesta, but in India it
becomes the drink of the gods : the change is
analogous to that of the Greek nectar. Other de-
velopments on Indian soil we need not chronicle. It
will be observed that here as in many other respects
the Indian tribes, migrating into a tropical climate
and all the differing conditions of a new country,
have changed the character of their Aryan inheritance. We do not find it easy to name an Aryan
cult which the Iranians have altered and the Indians
have left alone. That Lehmann wrongly cites the
Avestan Verethraghna we have already seen. The
myth of Yama (Av. *Yima,* according to what is presumably the Later Avestan form) is a somewhat

better case, though not very decisive. In the Rigveda
Yama and his sister Yamī, children of Vivasvant (Av.
Vīvahvant) are the first human pair. It is easy to
equate the name with *yama* "twin," and assume that
the myth made mankind start from twin "children
of heaven"—that *one* of every pair of twins was
among primitive peoples imagined to be a child of
the sky has been abundantly shown in Dr Rendel
Harris's researches on the cult of the Dioscuri. This
conjecture is borne out by the name of Yama's father,
which may well be a cult-epithet of the bright sky,
"shining abroad" (from the root *vas*, "to shine").
In India Yama subsequently became King of the
Dead, a conception which Parsism clearly could not
have used. But it is probably not Aryan : Yama's
posthumous royalty is only like that of Minos
among the Greeks, and it is a serious difficulty when
we bring in the Iranian factor. In the Avesta *Yima*
χšaẹta, "Yima the bright,"—Firdausi's Jamshîd,
familiar to readers of FitzGerald's Omar—is no
longer the first man : the Bundahish sets him in the
fifth generation, and it is probably dependent on lost
Avestan texts, for our Avesta has very clearly abandoned what seems to have been the Aryan view of him.
But now we must note that as early as the Gâthâs
we read of Yima's *sin*. In *Ys.* 32 [8], according to Bartholomae's version, which solves best the difficulties
of the passage, Zarathushtra says : " To these sinners

belonged, as fame tells, Yima also, son of Vīvahvant,
who desiring to satisfy mortals gave our people portions of cow's flesh to eat." In the context the
Daēvas are said to have deprived men of immortality
by deception. It is very clear that the Prophet is
referring to an already existing myth. Its points of
contact with the Fall-story in Genesis are temptingly
suggestive. Yima reigns over a community which
may well have been composed of his own descendants,
for he lived yet longer than Adam. To render them
immortal, he gives them to eat forbidden food, being
deceived by the Daēvas. What was this forbidden
food? May we connect it with another legend
whereby at the Regeneration Mithra is to make men
immortal by giving them to eat the fat of the *Ur-kuh*,
the primeval Cow from whose slain body, according
to the Aryan legends adopted by Mithraism, mankind
was first created? It is perhaps possible (see pp. 47,
55) that Zarathushtra made Mithra a chief among
the Daēvas. If so, he used the old saga to show that
the first man sinned by presumptuously grasping at
immortality for himself and mankind, on the suggestion of an evil power, instead of waiting for
Ahura's good time. Yima's punishment, according to
a legend which is difficult to dovetail with the story in
the second Fargard of the Vendîdâd (pp. 154 ff.), was
the loss of the " Kingly Glory " (χ*arenah*). Yima's
Paradise we refer to when we come to the

Vendîdâd *l.c.* Has this story, with its many incon-
sistent elements, owed anything to Babylon? Our
reconstruction is beset with too many uncertainties,
of translation and interpretation and comparative
mythology, to allow us the luxury of being dogmatic;
but the possibility must be noted. One more in-
congruity in the Yima-saga may be referred to as
significant in a different way, the epithet "good
shepherd" that clings to him still in the Yashts.
The Iranian Adam is not like Tennyson's "grand old
gardener": he takes after Abel, the "keeper of
sheep." Lehmann couples this with the extraordinary
sanctity of the Cow, which of course survived in
India, and the equally striking Iranian veneration of
the Dog. They are survivals from the nomad life on
the plains, adapted to their strangely different environment with as great or as little success as the
relics of naïve animism that come down from a
higher antiquity still.

We need not further elaborate our delineation of
the *milieu* in which the Prophet began his work. It
is obvious that we have done very little to describe
the Iranians after their Indian kin left them, during
a period which when Zarathushtra came may have
lasted a thousand years or more. If we have made
our principles clear, it will be seen that we have a
method for our exploration of the earlier period
which fails us for the later. The reader may perhaps

be incredulous when we assert the probability that
the Iranian period differed very little from the Aryan.
But slowness of change in a people remaining in the
same country, and unfertilised by foreign influences,
notoriously exhibits astonishing results. We have in
our own time watched the swift awakening of Japan
under the touch of the West, and we are seeing
China similarly shaking off a changelessness which
has lasted as long as the annals of civilisation.
Another illustration we have used already in this
chapter, the extraordinary faithfulness with which
in Lithuania the language, culture and religion of
the primitive Indo-European period were preserved
up to the fifteenth or sixteenth century of the
Christian era. On these analogies we should expect
to find that what changes Iranian culture underwent
during the period of its separate existence were
almost entirely limited to those caused by foreign
influence, which for this purpose means Babylonian.
We have already indicated two or three points
in which Babel may have touched the Bible of
Zoroastrianism. Two more suggestions of this kind
may be added from Hermann Oldenberg, as endorsed
by Schrader. He thinks the great Light-gods were
borrowed from Sumerians or Semites, or at least got
their astronomical character there. Mithra is the
only one with whom we are concerned (see above,
p. 37). The remark has mainly to do with the seven

Âdityas of the Veda, whom Oldenberg (*Religion des Veda*, p. 193) makes ultimately to come from the sun, moon and five planets. This presumes Babylonian influence in the Aryan period ; but it must be contended that the link between the Âdityas and their supposed Iranian congeners is very feeble. Lehmann denies it altogether, and he seems to be right. Another Aryan conception is claimed by Oldenberg as of foreign origin, that of Skt. Rta = Av. *Aša*, the universe as an ordered whole. Apart from the fact that the equation is not quite exact, the recognition of this astronomico-philosophical idea in the Aryan period can hardly be claimed as a certainty. A Babylonian connexion which, unlike these of Oldenberg, will belong to the Iranian period, is suggested by the statement of Herodotus (I. 131) that the Persians had learnt from Assyrians and Arabs to sacrifice to Οὐρανίη. This will refer to the cult of Anâhita, whose points of contact with the great Semitic goddess Ishtar and her kin will appear when we describe her Yasht (see also above, pp. 37 f.).

We have dwelt at length upon the religion of the pre-Reformation epoch because of its bearing upon the work of the Reformer himself. But we need to understand it also because of what we may call the Counter-reformation, which produces much the largest part of the Avestan poetry, the Yashts and analogous

matter in Yasna and Vendîdâd. Of this we shall not
speak more fully here. Our general picture will
suffice to show the relatively high religious position
of the people to whom Zarathushtra preached, and
the plastic character of the material he moulded into
a shape so novel in accordance with his own profound and original mind.

NOTE.—It is right to notice that the suggestion made here
(pp. 37, 43, and 55 f. below) as to Mithra's real origin and standing
in Zarathushtra's system is an individual's hypothesis only, presented with all diffidence as a possibility. It has not convinced
Prof. Williams Jackson. Bartholomae agrees with Oldenberg and
Hillebrandt in regarding Mithra as in Aryan times a sun-god.
Moreover Brugmann propounds a connexion between his name,
as meaning "friend," and the Latin *mītis*, Greek μειλίχιος.
Against this weight of authority we cannot plead here. We may
just quote Bartholomae's view that "in the strict Zarathushtrian
doctrine Mithra was not recognised as a divinity, as little as
Haoma; but as his worship was too firmly rooted among the
people, the priests were obliged afterwards to allow it." This is
not far from our theory that for Zarathushtra he was a Daēva.
For our view that Mithra was not the Sun we can quote the high
authority of Cumont: see p. 136, and pp. 224 n.[4], 225 n.[1], in
Cumont's *Textes et Monuments*.

CHAPTER V

ZARATHUSHTRA

THAT the Prophet's personality belongs to history we have already asserted (p. 15) : only the greatness of James Darmesteter's authority makes it necessary even to mention the doubt. *When* he lived and *where* he lived are very much harder questions, which we have no room to discuss here. The traditional dates of Zarathushtra's birth and death are 660 B.C. and 583 B.C. respectively. Since the appearance of Prof. Williams Jackson's classical paper "On the Date of Zoroaster[1]," this period has been largely accepted as approximately right : if anything can be settled by weight of authority, it will be hard to dispute a doctrine which has been accepted by F. Justi, L. C. Casartelli and E. W. West, even though Bartholomae holds out strongly for a "much higher" antiquity. The older doctrine, which put

---

[1] Published in the *Journal of the American Oriental Society* for 1896, and reprinted with additions in *Zoroaster*, pp. 150–81. The equally important companion paper, "Zoroaster's Native Place and the Scene of his Ministry," follows it in the same work.

Zarathushtra into the second millennium B.C., has been held by distinguished scholars, including formerly Prof. Williams Jackson himself; and the linguistic argument for bringing the Gâthâs nearer in date to the Veda is certainly powerful. Prof. Geldner (*Enc. Brit.* [11]xxi. 246—but contrast xxviii. 1041!) regards the fourteenth century B.C. as "most probable." We cannot be dogmatic: the primitive character of Gâthic language might be explicable by the fact that there was no migration into new territory—another application of the principle discussed above (pp. 31 f., 41, 45). Bishop Casartelli calls attention to the striking approximation of the traditional date to the times of Buddha, Confucius and Socrates. The sixth and fifth centuries B.C. were a period of immense importance in the religious history of the world.

Passing on thus ambiguously from the question When?, we ask the rather less important question Where? This again has been exhaustively discussed by Prof. Jackson (*op. cit.* p. 48 n. above). It seems possible to fix with fair certainty the region of his birth and early life as lying in Âdarbaijân. His mother Dughdhova's family seems to have been connected with Raghâ, a district which gave its name to the well-known town of Rhagae, named in the Book of Tobit and identified with Raï in Media, near Teheran. Personal names in his circle, by the way, are freely found. His father Pourushaspa is named

several times in the Avesta, and his clan-name
Spitama or Spitâma occurs very frequently.   His
daughter Pouruchista's marriage to Jâmâspa is the
subject of one of the Gâthâs.   These names are mentioned to illustrate the precision of the Avestan
notices, for all their scantiness serving well to bring
the man's real personality before us.   The names are
not of the stuff of which myths are made.   Spitama
means the same as the English White: Zarathushtra[1]
itself, like Frashaoshtra (p. 89), contains the word
uštra, "camel," just as Jâmâspa, Vîshtâspa and other
prominent names contain *aspa*, "horse."   The first
element in the Prophet's name is uncertain : perhaps
"old" (cf. γέρων) is as likely as any.   The ingenious
persons who turn all the prophets of mankind into
solar or other myths have in Zarathushtra's name
a problem worthy of their skill.   The place where
Zarathushtra first preached is much disputed, as the
tradition is evenly balanced.   Prof. Williams Jackson
is inclined to combine the two accounts by supposing
that he travelled to Eastern Iran (Bactria), and after
much discouragement, reflected in the Gâthâs, there
made his royal convert Vîshtâspa, returning later on
the full tide of success to press his propaganda in his
native land.   Whether Vîshtâspa reigned in Eastern

---

[1] The classical Ζωροάστρης, *Zoroaster*, appear to owe their form to
the mediation of Old Persian, as is the case with Ὡρομάσδης, Ἀρει-
μάνιος, and other special names of Zoroastrianism.

or Western Iran may be left uncertain : that he was
the Constantine of the new faith is one of the very
few historical facts emerging from the Gâthâs.   The
reappearance of the name Vîshtâspa—perhaps half a
century later, on Jackson's theory of the Prophet's
date—with the father of King Darius I is suggestive :
it may possibly link Darius's branch of the Achae-
menian family with the royal house in which the
Prophet first won recognition.   There are other
reasons for supposing Darius to have been the first
successor of Cyrus to hold a definitely Zarathushtrian
faith.   But this is a thorny question, which hardly
concerns us here.

Legend has added immensely to the scanty record
of the Prophet's life.   It is hardly necessary to refer
to the stories of the later literature, whose only value
lies in their throwing out in strong relief the simple
verisimilitude of the picture in the Gâthâs.   Two
only we will refer to, for special reasons.   One, which
was known to the Romans at least as early as Pliny
(*Nat. Hist.* VII. 15), was that "Zoroaster was the
only human being to laugh on the very day of his
birth."   It is tempting to recognise an earlier allusion
to this well-known story, in one of the most famous
passages in Roman literature.   At the end of the
Fourth Eclogue, Virgil thus apostrophises his
wondrous Babe :

> Incipe, parue puer, *risu* cognoscere matrem.

4—2

Assuming that this means "to greet thy mother with a smile"—and the alternative "by *her* smile" forces the Latin intolerably—we have at once a difficulty which seems to have escaped the commentators. The whole point of the passage is that the child is *new-born*—indeed, if Prof. Conway is right[1], not even that. And when did a new-born child laugh or even smile at anybody? Is not the poet here, as in so much of this mysterious poem, using Eastern imagery? "Risisse eadem die quo genitus esset unum hominem accepimus Zoroastrem," says Pliny, a century after the Eclogue was written. Virgil's Child should share that unique distinction. Indeed the remaining lines of the poem will gain point if we assume that Virgil, so diligent a reader of Greek literature, knew what Greek writers had told of Zoroaster generations before, his receiving laws in direct converse with the Deity. Virgil's conclusion,

Incipe, parue puer : qui non risere parenti [or parentis],
nec deus hunc mensa, dea nec dignata cubili est,

is in its first element well satisfied by this allusion, assuming the classical embellishment that the divinity not only instructed but feasted the sage. To bring

[1] *Vergil's Messianic Eclogue* (London, 1907), pp. 13 ff. Note Mr Warde Fowler's interesting citation from Suetonius in the same book (p. 71), showing that Virgil himself was believed at birth to have abstained from crying.

in the second point involves the assumption that the West had received another very prominent element in the Zoroaster-legend : that we have no evidence of this may be frankly confessed, but its absence is entirely natural. In the Yashts we read of Zarathushtra's wife Hvovi, a member of a noble family at Vîshtâspa's court. Two brothers of this family are named with their patronymic in the Gâthâs as conspicuous among Zarathushtra's disciples and helpers. He became the son-in-law of the one, Frashaoshtra Hvogva, and the father-in-law of the other, Jâmâspa Hvogva, whom he calls *saošyant*, "one who will deliver" men—a title especially belonging to himself. On this wholly natural basis later legend built a marvellous superstructure. Unfortunately we cannot fix the period, or tell whether there was authority for it in ancient Avestan texts[1]. According to this story, Zarathushtra has no children by Hvovi in the natural order, but they are to become the parents[2] of three sons who shall be born as the Regeneration draws near : the last of them, Saoshyant, is to bring

[1] The Bundahish undoubtedly depends largely on Avestan texts no longer preserved ; but if they were prose in this case, like the parts of *Yt.* 13 which are taken to allude to this story, we could not claim sufficient antiquity for them except in a tentative way.

[2] The manner of this supernatural generation may be seen in Darmesteter's quotations on *Yt.* 13⁶² (*S. B. E.* xxiii. 195) : any intelligent reader may judge of its resemblance to Matthew i, with which it has been solemnly compared !

about the final deliverance of creation from all evil. It is obvious that Hvovi might just as well be a goddess bride outright, and Virgil may very easily have heard the story in this form, which assimilates it to myths of Greece long familiar to him. If this conjecture is reasonable—and of course it is conjecture and no more—the promised birth of the Zoroastrian Messiah, who is to bring in the Age of Gold, becomes a most important element in the Oriental lore that gave the great poet his motive.

We pass on from this only too seductive pursuit of dim possibilities to describe the Prophet's doctrine, which we have to draw out of poems obscure enough in their diction, but eminently well preserved, and proceeding, we can hardly doubt, mainly from Zarathushtra himself, or at least his immediate followers : there seems to be no consideration of weight against the former alternative, which we shall assume henceforth in general. The individuality of Zarathushtra's mind comes out with vivid emphasis as we examine the environment in which he was brought up, and again as we trace in the later Avesta the development of Parsism after his day. There does not seem to be any kindred spirit in ancient Iran : Zarathushtra's brethren would be found rather in India. He is intensely abstract in his thinking. Anthropomorphism and nature worship, such as the earlier and later Aryans of both

branches practised, he tried to expel from religion
altogether. He was not content with merely ignoring
the old gods, so that Mithra and Anâhita, the Fravashis, Verethraghna and Haoma are never named
in the Gâthâs[1]. Most of these, with the "nameless
gods" of the sky and the light and the heavenly
bodies, were included among the Aryan *daivās*; and
it solves most simply the old problem of the fact that
Avestan *daēva* means "demon," if we assume that
Zarathushtra himself denounced the old "heavenly
ones" as evil powers, even as Hebrew prophets
denounced Baal and Ashtoreth. When the cult of
Mithra and his troop came back again, not very long
after the Prophet passed away, there was no Gâthâ
text to remind Zarathushtra's nominal followers that
Mithra was repudiated by the Founder. This may be
mere ignorance : lapse of time, or geographical separation from the first home of the Faith—one of which
causes at least must be postulated to account for
the linguistic differences between the Gâthâs and the
Later Avesta—would explain such a fundamental
misunderstanding of the doctrine. But the absence
of a Gâthâ to show explicitly who the Daēvas were
looks more like design than accident. The Gâthâs
were only preserved by priestly recitation in worship;
and priests who wanted to go on worshipping Mithra

[1] On Mithra see p. 47. Haoma is probably alluded to, though
not named : see p. 110.

were quite clever enough to forget a Gâthâ which denounced them expressly as *daēvayasna* for doing so. The coast was thus clear for reintroducing the Iranian nature-gods, whom the people (*teste Herodoto*) had never ceased to worship, regularising them by making them saints or angels : the process is familiar enough in the history of Christianity. Then *daēva* could continue to mean " demon," but denote only Angra Mainyu and his infernal crew, whom Zarathushtra himself had included under this title, the better to discredit the old gods.

Having thus discarded conceptions of Deity which failed to satisfy his spiritual sense, Zarathushtra proclaimed his own conceptions in their stead. One inherited name for God was good enough for him. *Ahura* in the Gâthâs already means " Lord," its etymological meaning "spiritual" having apparently died out before the division of the Aryans. Who or what was "the Lord"? His relation to Nature is wholly in accord with the Bible itself. "Who covereth Himself with light as with a garment" is almost a quotation from the Gâthâs. But his own nature is something higher yet. He is "the Wise" (*Mazdāh*), which seems specially to denote the "knowledge of good and evil," the unerring instinct that can distinguish between Truth and Falsehood, which for the Prophet were the most vital aspects of good and evil. Not only is this conception

free from material and external conceptions of God :
it is conspicuous for its ethical character. It is not
a speculative philosophy but a thoroughly practical
doctrine. Abstract and profound though Zarathushtra's thought was, he was characteristically
Iranian in his outlook—free from mysticism and
asceticism and dreaminess. "Wisdom" was very
much like the Old Testament conception, the gift
for which Solomon prayed. The attainment of
Wisdom lay through the characteristic stages of
"good thoughts, good words, good deeds," and for
Zarathushtra's disciple "good deeds" were not futile
sacrifices or vain austerities, but diligent tilling of
the soil, hatred of deceit and lying, and kindness to
the creatures of Ahura.

It is necessary to outline thus Zarathushtra's
ethics in order to understand his conception of God,
which was more closely bound up with conduct than
in any non-Christian religion. In the absence of
a recent discovery, for which see p. 73, we should
be inclined to regard this name "Wise" as Zarathushtra's own special revelation. The elements of
the combination Ahura Mazdâh in the Gâthâs are
declined as separate words, arranged indifferently,
and either word may be used alone. "The Wise
Lord" will probably represent it to us better than
"Ahura Mazdâh." It soon became fixed as a proper
name. By the time of the great Darius, the first

Zarathushtrian King of Persia (it would seem), the
name has become a single word, Auramazda, with
flexion only at the end.

We can only conjecture the motive of Zarathushtra's next step in the formulation of his doctrine
of God. The Gâthâs are crowded with allusions to
six highly abstract conceptions, which are known
collectively by the name *Ameša Spenta*, "Immortal
Holy Ones " (Persian *Amshaspands*). They (or some
of them) expressly share the divine title of *Ahura* ;
and it is by no means clear whether we should call
them archangels or actual parts of the divine essence.
It has been supposed that Zarathushtra was making
concession to human weakness, trying to supplant
polytheism by giving men a plurality of objects for
worship, which were only complementary attributes
of Deity. As we shall see, this was the result, but we
need not suppose that it was the design. "Archangel " is too humble a title for beings who actually
share adoration with Deity. We should be poly-
theists, not Christians, if we prayed to "God and
Michael and Gabriel." The analogy of the Trinity
comes much closer. The Ameshas are *within* the
Deity, essential parts of the divine hypostasis. If
the Apocalyptist was really borrowing imagery from
Zarathushtra when he wrote of "the seven spirits of
God " (Rev. iii. 1), he certainly fathomed the Iranian
Prophet's thought extraordinarily well. For Mazdâh

is sometimes one of the Ameshas, while at other
times his superiority to them is indicated by their
being set apart, often with Sraosha (p. 99) to make
up the number seven. We might even see this alternative in "the seven spirits which are before the
throne" (Rev. i. 4). But thorny questions of Apocalyptic exegesis are outside our present province, and
we must go on to examine Zarathushtra's doctrine.
Before taking up the Ameshas one by one, we
must observe that they are not wholly new conceptions. Each of them has a special province in the
material world, which in one case at any rate descends
with the Amesha's name itself from the Aryan period.
We may suppose the Reformer to have selected from
old inherited beliefs some which were capable of
adaptation to his system. While this implies some
amount of personification, traceable rarely in this
form within the Gâthâs themselves, we find the
divine names used perpetually as abstract nouns,
without any personification at all. One of the
greatest difficulties in the Gâthâs is that of deciding
when to put the initial capital in our rendering of
these words : the Germans have a great advantage
in having the choice made for them ! Thus in very
many places the word *ašā*, if taken as an instrumental case, may be either "with rightness, rightly,
duly," or "with the help of Rightness (Asha)"; and
in a fair proportion of them we could equally well

construe it vocative, " O Asha." An example of this
may be seen in a stanza quoted below (p. 87). We
might add that the personification is never very real.
Bishop Casartelli is quite justified in his insistence
upon the necessity of translating them : Asha and
Vohu Manah are the best renderings in the Later
Avesta, but they should always be "Rightness"
and " Good Thought" or the like in the Gâthâs.
Dr Casartelli goes on to compare Bunyan's per-
sonified virtues and vices. The comparison however
must be used cautiously, for Bunyan has no abstractions, even when his personification lasts only
for a line or two, and the Gâthâs have nothing else.
"Mercy" in the *Pilgrim's Progress* is much more of
a human being than most heroines in fiction ; while
Aramaiti has not flesh and blood enough to make a
goddess !

Proceeding to deal with the "Immortals" individually, we begin with Vohu Manah and Asha, who have
at all periods the closest association with Ahura. In
the Gâthâs Asha is nearer to him, but in the Later
Avesta he yields pride of place to Vohu Manah.
Asha has often the epithet *vahišta*, " best," which in
later times was stereotyped as part of his name. It
is used interchangeably with its positive *vohū* in the
Gâthâs as the epithet of *Manah*, "Thought," where
sometimes "Thy Thought" (addressing Mazdâh) serves
instead as the Amesha's name. The conception of

Asha is at least Iranian, if not older, for the name is identical with the Persian *Arta-*, which figures so constantly in proper names. Its relation to the Sanskrit *ṛtá* is not perfectly regular, but it is generally accepted as proving Aryan antiquity. Plutarch renders it ᾿Αλήθεια, and the Persian connotation of Truth was so wide that it represents Asha well enough. "Right," "Rightness," "the Divine Order," are equivalents as near as we can supply. Lehmann interprets Asha's connexion with Fire by assuming that he followed an old *Sondergott* of the ordeal fire. Like *aša*, *vohū manah* is a neuter, but comes nearer to personality by its meaning — "Good Thought," which is thought in accord with "the Wise Lord." As we have seen, this implies practical rightmindedness, which makes the Amesha's special connexion with cattle readily understood: the care of cattle is a distinguishing mark of Zarathushtra's good man. The common comparison with the Greek Logos is therefore at best only partial. Plutarch, who rendered Εὔνοια, "Goodwill," did not think of it.

Next comes "Sovranty" or "Dominion," χšaθra, in the Later Avesta linked with the adjective *vairya*, "desired," which may imply "according to divine Will." Plutarch renders εὐνομία. The association of this Amesha with metals, already hinted at in the Gâthâs, is connected by Prof. Jackson with the *ayah* χšusta, the flood of molten iron which is at last to purify the world. It will, we are told, burn up all evil, while the righteous will feel it like a bath of warm milk. (A writer in the *Athenæum* recently suggested that Orphism had been affected by this conception: the Orphic initiate felt "like a kid bathed in milk.") The conception is essentially eschatological, even as some are saying the Gospel "Kingdom of God" was in the thought of Jesus. Anyhow, whether the "Good Time Coming" is on this side or that side of the grave, the good Zarathushtrian could pray with us *ājamyāṭ χšaθrem θwem*, and mean what we do in the Lord's Prayer.

The fourth Amesha, whom we have already met with (p. 36) as an Aryan divinity, is of feminine gender like the remaining pair. The epithet *spenta*, which belongs to all the six, is specially appropriated to her, so that her name in later language is Spandaramat. It may be remarked that the Iranian idea of "holiness" is quite in keeping with the practical character of the religion. It is no cloistered virtue, divorced from conduct, but connotes *beneficence*. The divine attributes which meet in the circle of the Seven are all alike "holy" in that they promote the coming of the New Order, to which Ahura's whole creation moves. Aramaiti (*σοφία* in Plutarch) represents the man-ward side of what Khshathra describes on the divine side: God's Kingdom, and man's attitude of loyal devotion to it. Such a spirit may well have the attribute *spenta* in a peculiar sense. This understanding of Aramaiti as "piety" or "devotion" goes back to Aryan times, and attaches itself to an etymology which (whether right or wrong) was well set in the popular consciousness: it produced an antithesis *tarō-maiti*, "perverseness." Of course this product no more proves that Aramaiti originally meant "devotion" than Epimetheus proves that Prometheus meant "forethought"—to take the first parallel that strikes us. Now, according to Sāyaṇa, the greatest of ancient Indian commentators on the Rigveda, there is a Vedic passage where Aramati means the Earth. This must be entirely independent of the Avesta, where from the first there are strong traces of the same association. May we conjecture that two originally distinct words were fused by popular etymology in the Aryan period? *Arā mātar* is a possible Aryan name for Mother Earth: compare the old Greek ἔρα (ἔραζε, "earthwards") and the Germanic word from which our *earth* and German *Erde* are descended. (We might easily explain the added consonant by postulating conflation in Germanic between this name and that of the independent earth-deity *Nerthus*, of whom Tacitus tells us.) This seems a simpler link than those usually fashioned to connect the two ideas.

Last, we have a pair never found apart, Haurvatât and Ameretât, Health ("wholeness") and Immortality.

Their respective provinces may be seen in *Ys.* 51⁷, where "water and plants, Health and Immortality" are named together in a list of blessings. Professor Jackson notes "the primeval idea of the tree of life and the fountain of youth." There is very little specific lore about them. It is curious that Plutarch goes wholly astray with so simple an idea as that of Ameretât.

We cannot attempt to be exhaustive, and need say no more about Zarathushtra's Deity. The pure and lofty character of his concept will be obvious. It would be hard indeed to find any non-Christian idea of God so wholly free from unworthy elements. But the absence of the attributes of grace and love is by itself sufficient reason for the failure of Parsism to establish itself as a world-religion.

The other side of Zarathushtra's contribution towards the solving of the *Welträtsel* is found in his doctrine of Evil, which is fully as profound and as abstract as the side we have been studying. It is commonly denominated dualistic, a name it by no means deserves, unless Christianity is to bear the same reproach. Good and Evil are not co-ordinate and co-eternal Powers for him any more than for us. The superiority of Good is manifest throughout, and the triumph of Good at the last is as complete as it is in the Bible eschatology. It was difficult to be original in framing a doctrine of evil spirits. There

are few parts of the world where men would not have
regarded scornfully the hypothetical tone of Luther's
great defiance—

> And were this world all devils o'er,
> And watching to devour us—.

Iranian religion was less devil-ridden than most,
but it was well enough supplied to give the great
thinker all necessary hints. But Zarathushtra developed them in his own way. He taught how the
two primeval spirits in the beginning chose Good
and Evil respectively, and thereupon commenced an
antagonism that will not cease till the spirit of Evil
and they that are of his portion are finally destroyed.
Into this great strife men are to enter with heart and
soul, and by lives of purity, devotion, righteousness
and strenuous industry to assault perpetually the
kingdom of Evil. Zarathushtra continued to employ
a name which had come down from Aryan antiquity,
Druj, "Lie." That this was its earliest connotation
is suggested not only by the Old Persian noun *drauga*,
from the same root and with the same meaning, but
also by the German *Be-trug*. On the other hand,
Skt. *druh* means generally "to injure," while Schrader
notes from the other end of the Indo-European area
the Old Norse *draugr* and Old English *dréag*, meaning "ghost." Whether Schrader is right or wrong in
making malignant ghosts the root of the idea, the

Iranian meaning is not doubtful. It is a tribute to national character that all evil should be summed up in the she-devil "Deceit." Zarathushtra did not bring a new teaching to the Persians in his emphasis on Truth: the Reformation had in Herodotus' day but little permeated the classes whose education was summed up in the three famous divisions—riding, shooting, speaking the truth. The Prophet's special name for the spirit of evil was *Angra Mainyu*, "hostile spirit"—an idea exactly reproduced in "the Satan" of post-exilic Judaism, which very probably owes something to Parsism[1]. In the *locus classicus*, *Ys.* 30, a Gâthâ which has been described as a *Lehrgedicht*, a kind of catechism in verse, Zarathushtra calls "the Better and the Bad" spirits *twins*, which implies not merely their coexistence, but the fact that they are thought of only in their mutual relation —the thought of the one implies that of the other. There has been much discussion on the question whether Angra Mainyu is the direct antagonist of Mazdâh or of his "holy Spirit," Spenta Mainyu, who appears often in the Gâthâs. It will be sufficient here to repeat Geiger's judgement, cited with approval by Prof. Jackson (*Grundriss*, II. 648): "So far as Ahura Mazda is the positive, to which Evil makes the negative, he is called Spenta Mainyu; Evil or

[1] See the writer's article "Zoroastrianism" in Hastings' *Bible Dictionary*, IV.

its personification is Aṅra Mainyu or Aka Mainyu.
Spenta Mainyu and Aka Mainyu are thus called
twins (*Ys.* 30³), inasmuch as they do not exist independently, but each in relation to the other; they
meet in the higher unity Ahura Mazda. They exist
before the beginning of the world, but their opposition only comes to its expression in the world that
we see. Ahura Mazda is Creator of everything; but
when he creates anything as Spenta Mainyu, there
comes with it of itself the negative counterpart, or
as the poet puts it in popular form, 'Aṅra Mainyu,
the bad spirit, creates Evil in opposition to the
Good' (*Ys.* 30⁴ᶠᶠ·)." If Zarathushtra conceived of the
two spirits as alike proceeding from God, we may
recognise in his statement about their "choosing"
of good and evil a doctrine essentially identical with
that of the *fall* of Satan, made so familiar to us by
Milton[1]. In the antagonism of "holy" and "hostile"
spirits we recall what has just been said of the meaning of *spenta*, which marks Mazdâh's Spirit as the
friend and helper of man and creation, while the
other spirit is their enemy. Zarathushtra's name for
the fiend ultimately predominated, the Druj being
specialised in the Later Avesta. But she left an

---

[1] See on the whole subject Casartelli's *Mazdayasnian Religion under
the Sassanids* (Bombay, 1899), pp. 1–71. Prof. Jackson denies that
Ahriman is a fallen angel (*Grundriss*, II. 649); and he now regards
the two principles as distinct and separate.

interesting trace behind. The Persian Ahriman and
the Greek 'Αρειμάνιος presume in Old Persian (from
which, and not from Avestan, we have seen the
Greeks received the Zoroastrian names) a form
*Ahrimanyuš, instead of *Ahramanyuš, the equi-
valent of the Avestan. This involves, it would seem,
that the name was treated as *feminine*, the influence
of the Druj thus persisting when the name has been
supplanted[1].

With Angra Mainyu as their chief Zarathushtra
associated the Daēvas. Their original character has
been discussed already. Assuming our results, we
may suppose that he put them with Angra Mainyu
as spirits of *deception*, drawing men away from the
true God and eternal life. Hardly any Daēvas are
individually named in the Gâthâs, beyond those already described; but there is one of them who must be
introduced here, Aēšma, "Wrath" (cf. οἶμα, Lat. *ira*).
In later times he specially represented "drunken
rage," and the name *daēva* was appended so as to
make a single word in the Persian language: hence the
fiend 'Ασμοδαῖος in *Tobit*. In the Median folk-story
which may be presumed to be the basis of that book[2]

[1] That Ahriman and the Greek name presume a feminine form in
Old Persian was urged by the present writer in a paper published in
1892. Bartholomae's assumption that a by-form *Ahriya-* is implied
seems much less probable.

[2] See the writer's paper in *Expository Times*, March 1900, or more
briefly in Hastings' *Dict. Bib.* iv. 989.

Asmodaeus played a rather different part, probably because that story comes from a distinct stratum of Iranian life (see p. 77). Human members of the Satan's host include of course the *daēvayasna*, unbelievers who worship the Daēvas, otherwise viewed as *dregvatō*, "men having the Druj," as opposed to *ašavanō*, "men having Asha": they are "those who love and make a lie." Various tribes and individuals are named in the Gâthâs as thus hostile to the Religion: we should name especially the *Kavayō*, the chiefs who maintained the unreformed religion, the *Usijō* and *Karapanō*, its priests and teachers. Creatures of Angra in a lower scale are *χrafstrā*, "wild beasts," a term which even in the Gâthâs is extended to include all that robs and ravens, Daēvas and men alike. The list of demons grows in later times.

It remains to describe Zarathushtra's eschatology, the part of his system which on the whole suffered least from the counter-reformation of later days. The individualist side of the picture will be presented subsequently (pp. 159 f.), as developed by poets and thinkers of the generations following the Prophet. It is perhaps risky to trust general impressions where the material is so scanty and so obscure as it is in the Gâthâs, but we cannot mistake Zarathushtra's pre-eminent concern with the bearing of eschatology on conduct, and with the victory of all that is good in the world when the long struggle with evil comes

to its climax.   He looks forward to a "Great Crisis,"
a day of reckoning when men's lives shall be finally
weighed, and the followers of Asha shall have their
reward.   The followers of the Druj shall go for ever
to the House of the Druj:—

Whoso cometh to the Righteous One, far from him shall be the
future long aeon of misery, of darkness, ill food and crying of woe.
To such an existence, ye followers of the Druj, shall your own Self
bring you by your actions (*Ys.* 31²⁰, after Bartholomae).

What is involved in the *daregēm āyū* is a question
essentially like that over which Christian expositors
have differed so much in the rendering of the Greek
"aeon" which we have used to translate it.   The
word in both languages (as in Latin *aevom*) may be
applied to the term of a human life, which was probably its earliest meaning.   But there can be little
doubt that the connotation of the word in Avestan
as in Hellenistic was in such contexts that of time
without visible horizon.   The universalist conception,
by which the *ayah χšusta* (see pp. 61 f.) will burn up
the evil and so purify evil beings, may well have
been outside Zarathushtra's thought.   But there remain at any rate two unreconciled anticipations of
annihilation and of penal suffering, as the future of
the wicked after death, which co-exist in the Gâthâs,
much as they do in the New Testament, and later
Parsi theology was left to harmonise them if it could.
After all, they were alike but figures, by which in

different moods the Prophet expressed his conviction
of a Theodicy—that one day it would be well with
the righteous and ill with the wicked, a final and
complete reversal of the unequal justice that this life
so often metes out to them; and if in a matter lying
beyond direct vision he only saw in a mirror riddle-
wise, we need not be too careful to remove his in-
consistency, remembering the "reverent agnosticism"
which must very largely condition our own thought
on the problem of retribution.

Very prominent in Zarathushtra's doctrine of the
Last Things is *cinvatō peretu*, "The Bridge of the
Separater." Over it he promises to conduct the pious
into the "House of Song," *garō demāna*, where God
dwells for ever with His own. It is likely enough
that this was an old myth, originating perhaps with
the rainbow, which lent itself to the Prophet's ethical
purpose. In later conceptions—whether starting
from the earlier age or not we have no means of
divining—the Bridge was broad for the righteous,
narrow as a razor for the wicked, who fell off it into
hell: Islam borrowed this idea in the well-known
Arch of Al-Sîrât. The "Separater" or Judge may
have been Rashnu, the *yazata* with the scales, who
weighs the good and evil in each life and gives his
verdict on the balance. But it is probably significant
that Zarathushtra does not name him: he does not
seem anxious to add to the number of spiritual beings

whose names may stand among the angels of Ahura.
That a man's Self is his own determinant of destiny
is the one doctrine that matters.

One more technical term of the eschatology calls
for comment, the *frašōkereti* or "advancement" of
the world of life: the abstract noun does not appear
till the Yashts, but the verbal phrase is prominent in
the Gâthâs—see for example *Ys.* 30⁹ (below, p. 95).
The machinery whereby the Regeneration is to be
achieved has been already described, and it will be
apparent that any who expect prosaic consistency or
a sharply defined mental picture of the future will be
disappointed. It is without form and void, as Apocalyptic is wont to be when studied by unsympathetic
minds. But the ideas of Prophets are at least as
worthy of study as crabs or even stars; and old-world
eschatological dreams are at the present moment
exacting very special attention from various students
of human thought. We do well to make some effort
to realise the figures that loomed for Zarathushtra
out of the mists of the dim future. They were des-
tined, it would seem, to exercise extraordinary influence upon the world of the next millennium, and
through that world upon our own. Are we justified
in claiming Zarathushtra's right to be acknowledged
as the founder of Apocalyptic? It is too large a
question to answer here in any adequate way, but
we may briefly recognise the strong probability that

contacts with a Zoroastrianised Persia did much to stimulate in Israel the growth of a form of literature which from the Maccabaean era downwards dominated Jewish thought and created the *milieu* of the Gospel proclamation. This fact alone, even if the proof of contact between Parsism and Judaism were held to be insufficient, gives a profound modern interest to the visions of the Sage of Iran. Others before him dreamed of a paradise, a very earthly paradise indeed. He was the earliest thinker to make it ethical. He saw no houris and no winecups in his abode of bliss. He "looked for a new heaven and a new earth, wherein dwelleth Righteousness." We have quoted the very latest-written words of the Christian Scriptures to be a summary of his ideal; and thereby we have only paid just tribute to the moral grandeur of this dim figure from the distant past—a man who believed in God and believed therefore in the Triumph of Good, and taught men by this great Hope to guide the life of every day.

NOTE.—Hommel's discovery of the name *Assara Mazas* in an Assyrian record of the middle of the second millennium B.C. takes the divine name back to the Aryan period, or to Iranian antiquity prior to the change of *s* to *h* (cf. p. 9). The Boghaz-keui *Indra* and *Nâsatia* might be Indo-Aryan, but *Mazas* cannot. It seems probable therefore that Mazdâh was a cult epithet of a great *Ahura*—some would say the Vedic Varuṇa—long before Zarathushtra. This must apparently dispose of the otherwise more probable view referred to on p. 57.

CHAPTER VI

AFTER ZARATHUSHTRA

As the history of religion everywhere leads us to expect, the Reformer's victory over lower forms of faith was only partial. A counter-reformation set in before the Gâthic dialect ceased to be spoken. The prose "Gâthâ of Seven Chapters" (*Haptanghaiti*— *Ys.* 35–42) shows us the old nature deities back again ; and it is not likely that their adorers laid much stress on the fine distinction between polytheism and angelolatry. The Gâthâs continued to be chanted in the divine service, but they must have been difficult even when their dialect was still familiar. When the interpretation of them fell more and more into the hands of the priests, and the Gâthic was to the masses of the people exactly what Latin is in Romance countries to-day, there was nothing left to check polytheism, till the systematisation of orthodox Parsism under the Sassanian kings. Had the Gâthâs not been preserved, we should have recognised very little in the Yashts to set in a different class from what we find in the Rigveda.

As we must examine the Yashts in some detail later on, we need say no more now on this side of the degeneration which marks the centuries between Zarathushtra and the Sassanians. Nor must we spare much space for the other side, which scarcely concerns us in our study of the verse parts of the Avesta : we will attempt for completeness' sake a brief summary of results without either argument or evidence, which would have to be rather technical.

The Magi are stated by Herodotus (I. 101) to have been one of the six tribes of the Medes. As one of the other tribes is called by him " Aryan," we may assume that the Magi were indigenous in a country where the Aryans were immigrant conquerors. They may well have been a sacred caste, analogous to the Brahmans in India. Darius in his great inscription at Behistan tells how Gaumâta the Magus, when Kambujiya (Cambyses) was in Egypt, personated the king's murdered brother Bardiya (Smerdis), and raised a revolt. Herodotus tells the story with embellishments ; and he gives us the significant statement that the triumphant conspiracy of Persian nobles under Darius, which set him on the throne, was commemorated by the annual festival of the *Magophonia*, a sort of Fifth of November. It looks like an attempt of the native population to shake off the Persian yoke, and one that came near success: the pretenders, the expiation of whose "lie" is recorded on the Behistan Rock, may well have been insurgents in the same cause. If we read the history aright, the Magi waited their time and gradually won compensation in spiritual power. The people, nominally conformed to Zarathushtra's religion, were ready enough to accept them as priests, and it would not be long before the upper classes followed suit. It is easy to see how a syncretism thus arose, with religion increasingly under the direction of priests who could use the opportunities well for bringing in their own doctrines and cults. They did not introduce their own unpopular name into the sacred texts that grew up under their inspiration[1]: it was left to foreigners like the Greeks to suit names to facts, and give the Magi the credit they deserved for the upgrowth of a virtually new religious system. In two very important matters even the Greeks retained the consciousness that the Magi had to be distinguished from the Persians. One of them ultimately established itself in Parsism, and is a conspicuous feature of the customs of Parsis to-day. The *Dakhmas*, or "Towers of Silence," on which the bodies of the dead are exposed till the vultures have stripped the skeleton bare, have their place in the

[1] Except in one passage—an exception proving the rule.

Vendîdâd, but were certainly not known in Persia under the Achaemenid kings. It was an aboriginal custom, described by Diodorus as characteristic of a barbarous people called Oreitae, dwelling in Baluchistan: see Schrader in *Enc. Relig.* II. 16. The other, which equally staggered the Greeks, was the practice of marriage between the closest kin—according to the Magian theology a religious duty of the most extravagant sanctity. It is, however, at least open to the gravest doubt whether this can be traced in the Avesta; and of course modern Parsis vehemently repudiate the idea that it ever formed a recognised element in their creed or practice. To these we may probably add, as characteristic of the Magi but not of Parsism, the "science" of astrology, the practice of magic—named from them—and divination by dreams. We might mention here that there seems reason to suppose the Book of Tobit to be a Jewish reconstruction of an old Median folklore story which in many features still preserves characteristics of Magian, not Zarathushtrian, doctrine and custom (cf. p. 68).

Into the Avesta the Magi brought, to speak generally, the elements which we find in the Vendîdâd. The Gâthâs are almost as innocent of ritual as the New Testament: like prophets elsewhere, Zarathushtra seems to have cared little for outward forms of worship. The Magi supplied the omission,

and it suffices to record with sincere relief that
their book of offices is in prose. They hardened the
Prophet's profound adumbrations of truth into a
mechanical system of dogma, therein showing the
usual skill of priests in preserving the letter and
destroying the spirit. Zarathushtra's doctrine of
Evil was developed into a systematic division of
the world between Ahura Mazdâh and Angra
Mainyu. Every angel and every creation of the
former had its exact counterpart in the infernal
order. The fact that the ingenious process was not
always completed may be evidence of the limitation
of Magian influence during the formative period of
Parsism. The Amesha Spentas are only perfunctorily
provided with fiends to match. It is a suggestive
fact that "Yasht 22," the general lines of which we
have tried to present in modern form below (pp. 159 ff.),
appears as a fragment : something sealed the lips of
the dogmatic interpolator as he tried to spoil the
lovely picture of the good man's soul entering heaven
with an exact counterpart describing the journey to
hell.

There is very much more which would have to be
said if our principal purpose were the description of
Persian religion as a whole. Limited as we are to
the poetical portions of the Avesta, we must pass by
the Sassanian reform, which unified and established
Parsi faith, the devastation that followed the coming

of Islam, the settlement in India and the modern history of the Parsi community. Similarly we must be content with naming two by-products of Persian thought which loom large in the early history of Christianity—the Parsi heresy of Manichaeism, and the most important and long victorious cult of Mithra, the latter seemingly a direct descendant of unreformed Iranian religion, scarcely touched by Zarathushtra's ideas, but considerably mixed with indigenous elements from the countries where it took its rise.

CHAPTER VII

THE GÂTHÂS: LITERARY FEATURES

FOR us as much as for the Parsis the kernel of the Avesta is to be found in the Gâthâs, which we are briefly reviewing in general before we proceed to take them in detail. They were the only part believed to come immediately from Zarathushtra, and as such they had a unique sanctity, which was doubtless enhanced very early by the rapid loss of the key to their meaning. Their dialect, as we have seen, was quite distinct from that of the Later Avesta; and even if they had been normalised—a very easy process which was actually applied several times when quotations were made—their obscurity would not have been materially lightened. To this we return presently. The title *Gāθā* claims our attention first. The word is Aryan, for Sanskrit gives us *Gāthā* (with *th* as in "hot*h*ouse"—the Avestan *θ* is a spirant like *th* in "*th*in"). Originally the name presumes poetical form, but when the reverence of a later age canonised

them, surrounded with the glamour of antique diction
and archaic dialect, their name began to be applied
to all ancient sacred writing that was clothed in the
same language.   Hence we have the name Gâthâ
given to seven short compositions in prose, the
changed religious position of which we noted above
(p. 74).   A paragraph may be quoted here from
Professor Geldner's brief account of the Avestan
literature in *Grundriss d. iran. Philologie* (II. 29):—

> The term Gatha is probably not to be understood according
> to its etymology simply as "song" or "hymn." We must re-
> member that in India the term *gât'ā* is often used in a technical
> sense. Among the Brahmans as among the Buddhists it denotes
> verses scattered about in narrative prose, which either form an
> integral part of the narrative or are attached to the prose and
> recapitulate its contents in concise phrase which it was easy to
> remember. By their form they were peculiarly adapted for oral
> transmission, and were perhaps originally designed for that end.
> Often they have become detached from the accompanying prose,
> and have been preserved alone without it.   If we might postulate
> similar conditions for the Gathas of the Avesta, these would like-
> wise presuppose a lost substratum of prose, for which the Gathas
> supplied introduction, *résumés* and *aperçus*. In favour of this
> stands their peculiar structure, their for the most part uniform
> arrangement, and the continuous line of thought within the
> closely-connected unity of each separate stanza. Many stanzas
> (e.g. *Ys.* 30³) point to a lost context by the presence of a demon-
> strative which finds no explanation in the text that precedes.

Geldner concludes that "we have preserved for us
in the Gathas the quintessence of instruction or

preaching which the oldest tradition put in the Prophet's mouth and left to be guarded in the circle of the faithful, his school and privileged followers." We compare with this the judgement of another great expert, that the Gâthâs are "Verspredigten," versified sermons (Bartholomae). That the Gâthâs were essentially esoteric lore, betrayed as such by frequent reference to "him that knows," the Gnostic for whom these deep things will be clear, we may accept from Geldner without necessarily agreeing with him that the polytheistic elements were allowed by the Prophet to survive in the outer circle.

There are however other reasons for the obscurity in question, of which we may name two, one of them doubtless applying mainly to foreigners studying a dialect long extinct, while the other probably operated almost as powerfully with those who first heard the hymns sung. The first of these depends on the conditions of Gâthic as a language peculiarly endowed with grammatical ambiguities. An excellent illustration is provided by Bishop Casartelli, when introducing to readers of the *Dublin Review* a verse translation of "The Plaint of the Kine" (*Ys.* 29). Of Bartholomae's *Die Gatha's des Avesta* he says :—

It impresses one with the almost hopeless divergence of views of even the most qualified experts, when we find what strange discrepancies of translation each new attempt produces. Thus in the very first verse of this Gâthâ a word which hitherto has been universally accepted as a substantive, and variously rendered as "drought" (Justi), "evil, prey" (Darmesteter), "desolation" (Mills), "filth" (Kanga), is by Bartholomae construed as the perfect of a verb meaning "to oppress"; and in verse 7 a word hitherto taken as an adjective meaning "sixfold" is by him treated as a substantive meaning "milk"! In both cases I have with considerable hesitation followed him.

We shall meet with many other illustrations as we go through the Gâthâs. The ambiguities of Gâthic arise from various causes, one of which may be mentioned as a sample. Through the Aryan fusion of *a*, *e* and *o* into the single vowel *a*, and the Gâthic indiscriminate lengthening of all final vowels (see pp. 12, 23 above), such a word as *barā* might answer to the Greek φέρω (indic. or subj.) or φέρε, or[1] to φόρε, φόρω (the lost instrumental), φόρω (dual), or again to the feminine φορά, or a neuter plural nominative. Needless to say all these alterations do not coexist in all such words, or indeed in this one, but these are typical. Vedic Sanskrit might be quite as ambiguous, but it has the advantage of an immensely larger literature by which to check results, while it has also a much more reliable native tradition. Phonetic change has moreover been more active in Iranian than in Indian speech, in certain directions

---

[1] Putting aside a disputed question whether it should not in this case be *bārā*.

which tend specially to produce confusion of originally different words.

The other source of obscurity to be mentioned here arises from the extraordinarily abstract character of Zarathushtra's thought. The Ameshas in particular are responsible for a great deal of ambiguity. Thus when we meet with the word *ašā* (cf. pp. 59 f. above) we must start with a problem of parsing—is it vocative or instrumental, the latter perhaps used by a peculiar syntax as a nominative? And then we want to know whether it is the personification or the common noun, and which of finely shaded meanings applies best to the passage before us. The perpetual recurrence of these shadowy abstractions not only makes the language difficult, but robs it of literary distinction. Of course, if Geldner's suggestions given above be accepted, we can hardly expect this quality. Versified summaries of the most eloquent sermons, composed to help the faithful to retain their essence in the memory, have almost as little chance of rising into literature as the mnemonic stanzas by which at school we painfully acquired the mysteries of Latin genders.

" Almost "—for after all the Prophet was in deadly earnest, and he preached on great themes, and spiritual fervour can make literature *malgré lui*, even under such unfavourable surroundings. We close this section with two extracts that have a beauty of their own, while not pretending that it would be easy to match them with more.   Zarathushtra's glory does not need any forced extension of his claims, and prophets are rarer than poets after all.

First then we cite *Ys.* 31 [7, 8] :

He that in the beginning thus thought, " Let the blessed realms be filled with lights," he it is that by his wisdom created Right.   Those realms which the Best Thought shall possess, thou dost glorify through thy spirit, O Lord, who art evermore the same.

I conceived of thee, O Wise One, in my thought, that thou, the First, art also the Last—that thou art Father of Good Thought, for so I apprehended thee with mine eye—that thou didst truly create Right, and art the Lord to judge the deeds of life.

Are the " happy spaces " those of the visible skies or the Paradise where the good shall dwell at last ? The former gives us a fine parallel to Kant's famous saying about the starry heavens and the moral law— the thought which united, if it did not originally produce, the two halves of the nineteenth Psalm.   If the eschatological thought is uppermost, we can appreciate the grandeur of the conception of Him who " prepared the kingdom " for His own " before the foundation of the world," and by His unchanging purpose has been preparing it ever since then—He the First and the Last, who inspires Religion, frames the Moral Law, and at last by it shall " judge the world in righteousness." Thoughts lofty as these could not express themselves in language that fell short of poetry.

Next we might quote the Prophet's musing on the mystery of Nature :—

This I ask thee, tell me truly, O Lord. Who is by generation the father of Right at the first [i.e. the Divine Order, or perhaps collective, the ordered Kosmos]? Who determined the path of sun and stars? Who is it by whom the moon waxes and wanes? This, O wise One, and yet more am I fain to know.

This I ask thee, tell me truly, O Lord. Who upheld the earth beneath and the firmament from falling? Who the waters and the plants? Who yoked swiftness to winds and clouds? Who is, O Wise One, creator of Good Thought [possibly also collective, the pious]?

This I ask thee, tell me truly, O Lord. What artist made light and darkness? What artist made sleep and waking? Who made the morning, the noon and the night, that call the understanding to their duties? (*Ys.* 44³⁻⁵.)

We had marked a stanza in a later hymn, but the doctors disagree so badly in the proper treatment of certain weak points in its interpretation, that it seems safer to leave it, and proceed to our analysis of the Gâthâs in detail.

CHAPTER VIII

CONTENTS OF THE GÂTHÂS

THE first hymn in *Gāθā Ahunavaitī* (*Ys.* 28) is one of a rather general character, and has few features on which we need tarry. The metre, as throughout the seven hymns of this Gâthâ, consists of three lines with 7 + 9 syllables each. Gâthic metre has been generally described already, but it may be worth while to make a fairly exact transcript of a specimen stanza, the opening one, in a literal translation :—

> With hands outstretched entreating
>   for support, I will pray, O Mazdâh
> first of all things for his works,
>   the holy Spirit's works, O Rightness,
> wherewith I may please the Will
>   of Good Thought and the Soul of the Kine.

Whether the Gâthic original had any more rhythm than our English we cannot tell : nothing has been discovered beyond what the student of prosody

might recognise in the version, a fixed number of
syllables in each line. The stanza presents us with
a bizarre conception which needs explanation. *Gēuš
urvan* is "Soul of Kine" among scholars who try
to be literary : for some unassignable reason "kine"
is acknowledged to be nearer to poetry than its
singular, which answers more exactly to *gēuš*, a
phonetic equivalent of Latin *bovis* and our *cow's*.
The gender however is indeterminate. As was
pointed out above (p. 44), Aryan veneration for
the indispensable Ox or Cow is a survival of the
days when the Aryans were nomads on the plains.
Its animistic deification is very natural among a
people who instinctively bowed before the creature
that made their plough go. "Who killed the
Ur-kuh?" (p. 43) is a question not quite easy to
answer. In Mithraism it is Mithra himself, who is
represented in every sculpture seated on the bull's
back, plunging the blade into its neck. The creative
and the regenerating results of the action form the
subject of the Mithraic mysteries. On the other
hand we might be sure the Daēvas would be credited
with what seems *primâ facie* an unfriendly act
towards the Cow. In either case the deified soul of
the primeval ox or cow will be the most natural representative in heaven of the spirit of agriculture
that was so dear to Zarathushtra. The rest of *Ys.* 28
is a prayer for enlightenment, grace and zeal to work

in the light of future blessedness. One stanza may
be quoted as typical :

> Spirit-of-Holiness ! when shall I face to face
> Thee and the Good-Mind see, and bounteous Ahura's throne,
> And the Divine Obedience ?   Through this sacred prayer
> May we in might ward off the wicked by our tongue !

So renders Dr Casartelli, observing that the last line
might be " *convert* the wicked."   This agrees with
Bartholomae's translation, "By this word (of promise)
we would convert the ruffians to that which is
greatest."   It is worth marking in view of the
Prophet's more normal attitude towards the enemies
of the faith, which is essentially that of the Imprecatory Psalms : such an utterance as Ps. cxxxix. 21, 22
could be very easily matched in the Gâthâs.   Following on this (the fifth) stanza there comes a general
prayer of the community, with phrases that seem to
exclude the direct authorship of Zarathushtra himself.   " Give to Zarathushtra and to us strong support," " O Aramaiti, give to Vîshtâspa and to me our
desire," and again " I pray for the best gifts, desiring
them for the hero Frashaoshtra and for myself, and
for those to whom thou wilt grant of the Good
Thought for all time ":—the speaker here must be
the faithful people, praying for their Prophet
himself, their king Vîshtâspa, the prime minister
Frashaoshtra (p. 50) and the community as a whole.

The " I " is accordingly collective, as so often in the
Hebrew Psalter and in modern hymns, but the express mention of Zarathushtra shows that it is a
disciple and not the Master who composes the hymn.
So at least we should imagine, but it is fair to say
that Bartholomae assumes the Prophet to be speaking
in the last stanza. This, as will be seen, is appropriate enough ; but there is no difficulty in its
utterance by the disciples. It runs thus in
Casartelli's version :—

> That by these laws I may for all eternity
> The grace of Holiness preserve and the Good-Mind, do Thou
> Teach me, from Thine own soul, by Thine own mouth, to preach
> Those laws whereby the world primeval first was made.

Here again we have to chronicle a serious difference between our authorities. *Aṅhuš pourvyō bavaṭ*
is translated as above by Mills and Casartelli in
accordance with the tradition. But Bartholomae
renders "how it will be with the First Life." The
verb may be future as well as past, and Bartholomae
makes "the first life" mean "life in this world,
before death," also called "corporeal life" or "this
life": its antithesis is "the future" or "second"
or "spiritual life." According to this attractive explanation, the preacher asks for inspiration that he
may set forth the way in which this life may be so
lived as to lead on to another.

The second hymn is a much more remarkable
composition than the first. It is a dialogue in
heaven, the interlocutors in which are variously
given. Chief among them in any case is *Gēuš
urvan*, the deified "Ox-Soul" whom we described
just now. Ahura Mazdâh is also beyond question
among the speakers, and seemingly Vohū Manah and
Asha, and an enigmatical genius called *Gēuš tašan*,
"Creator of the Ox," who in earlier mythology may
very well have been Mithra himself: the tacit
ignoring of a spirit who had possibly become chief
of the *daēvas*, and the maintenance of a mythology
which could be adapted to the new purpose, are alike
characteristic. It is remarkable that Zarathushtra
intervenes in the heavenly debate. Justi found here
a reference to the doctrine of *fravashis* (pp. 142 ff.) :
"it is his angel" that thus converses with Ahura
and his closest attendant spirits. In a symbolic
poem like this we hardly need call in a doctrine
which is never alluded to in the Gâthâs elsewhere,
and was probably set aside by the Prophet as super-
stitious. Adopting Bartholomae's arrangement of
the hymn, we may summarise thus. The Ox-Soul
complains among the spirits who surround Ahura
that he (that is, his earthly fellows, the cattle themselves) receives no care or kindness from men. The
Ox-Creator takes up the appeal and pleads with
Asha, who naturally bears responsibility, as the

impersonation of things as they should be. Asha
acknowledges that there is no adequate protector :
Ahura only knows, and he must determine. So to
Ahura the Ox-Creator betakes himself with his
client, who is promptly reminded that he has no
locus standi—the cattle are only chattels, created
to serve the agriculturist. So the Ox-Soul turns to
Vohū Manah and asks who has been appointed by
the divine will to care for the pleaders. The response is the naming of Zarathushtra, " who alone
our commands hath heard." The Ox-Soul is not
grateful : he expected an effective protector, " one
that commands mightily," and not one armed only
" with the ineffectual word of an impotent man." At
this Zarathushtra breaks in with a fervent prayer to
the trinity of Spirits, Ahura, Asha and Vohū Manah,
that he may receive strength and dominion for the
protectorship that is assigned him, with men's
recognition of his appointment. The Ox-Soul is
satisfied : " O Lord, now is help ours : we will be
of the service of your like," i.e. simply " you divine
spirits," as Bartholomae takes it. The obscurity of
the poem lies very largely in a condition of ancient
dialogue verse, seen conspicuously in the manifold
interpretations of the "Song of Solomon," the loss
of indications standing outside the verse to show
by whom the utterances are successively spoken.
Despite this we can recognise dramatic effectiveness

in the method the Prophet takes for acknow-
ledging his own insufficiency for a task demanding
strength as well as wisdom ; and we can appreciate
the unquestioning faith with which he assumes, and
makes his clients assume, that Ahura's promise avails
for him against a world in arms.

Ys. 30 follows, and soon proves itself one of the
central expositions of the creed.   It will be advisable
to quote it in a complete form, as a specimen of a
Gâthâ and more particularly to exhibit the fundamental doctrines of the Prophet in his own words.

1.   Now will I proclaim to those who will the things that the
wise should remember, for hymns unto the Lord and prayers to
Good Thought ; the blessing also that through Right shall be seen
by the wise thinker, which is with the heavenly lights.

2.   Hear ye with your ears the best things ; behold them with
a clear-seeing thought, for decision between the two Beliefs, each
man for himself before the Great Consummation, bethinking you
that it may be accomplished unto our pleasure.

3.   Now the two primeval Spirits, who revealed themselves in
vision as Twins [see p. 66], are the Better and the Bad in thought
and word and deed.   And between these two the understanding
ones chose aright, the void of understanding not so.

We stop to note that in this doctrinally crucial verse
the pundits differ grievously.   Thus χᵛafnā, taken
above as = Lat. *somnō*, is rendered by Geldner "of
their own action, automatic"; and the same scholar
denies the traditional "twins" for *yēmā*, taking it as
"directors" (Skt. *yáma*, a charioteer, etc.), with "the

Better and the Bad" as a kind of object. Bartholomae here seems more satisfactory, but the uncertainty
should be registered.

4. And when these Spirits twain met in the beginning they
ordained Life and Not-life, and that at the end the worst existence shall be to the followers of the Lie, the best abode (?) to the
follower of Right.

Here Bartholomae takes *vahištem manō* to be "best
abode," i.e. paradise—a translation based on etymology (cf. Greek *μονή*). But "Best Thought" is
the meaning of the combination in hosts of passages;
and the name of the archangel does not seem forced
as a designation of heaven. *Humanah*, "Good
Thought," was one of the heavens through which
the righteous passed to the "House of Song."

5. Of these twain Spirits he that held to the Lie chose the
doing the worst things; the holiest Spirit chose Right, he that
clothes himself with the massy heavens as a garment.

Compare Ps. civ. 2. In *Yt.* 13³ the sky is Mazdâh's
"starry robe": the original recalls Aeschylus' *ἡ ποι-
κιλείμων νύξ*.

So likewise they that are fain to please the Wise Lord by
deeds of truth.
6. Between those twain the Daēvas chose not aright, for
infatuation came upon them as they took counsel together, so that
they chose the worst thought. Then they rushed together to
Violence, that they might enfeeble the world of man.

A ẹ̆šma ("violence") is a semi-personification: see above (pp. 68 f.) on Asmodaeus in *Tobit*. The word "rushed," *hēndvārentā,* illustrates a curious principle which is fixed in the Later Avesta, but at most only in germ in the Gâthâs, the setting apart of a complete series of synonyms, nouns and verbs, to be used when demoniacal creations are spoken of. The verb *dvar* is peculiar to *daẹ̆vas* and their kin, where *ay (eo, εἶμι)* is used for creatures of Ahura. The latter have "*heads*" (*vaγδana*), where demons and men and animals of their creation have "*pates*" (*kamereδa*), and so on.

7. And to him (i.e. mankind) came Dominion, Good Thought and Right; and Aramaiti gave continued life of their bodies, and indestructibility, so that by thy retributions through the (molten) metal [p. 61] he may be victorious over these (foes).

Aramaiti's connexion with the Earth accounts for her bestowing resurrection on those who sleep in her bosom.

8. So when there cometh the punishment of these evil ones, then, O Wise One, at thy command shall Good Thought establish the Dominion in its fulness for those, O Lord, who deliver the Lie into the hands of Right.

9. So may we be those that make the world advance! O Wise One and ye other Lords [*Mazdåscā Ahurånhō,* lit. "ye Mazdâh Ahuras"] and Right, gather together the assembly, that thoughts may meet where Wisdom is at home.

A very hard stanza, in which we have specially taken into account Justi's criticism of Bartholomae. The

"advancement" of the world (mankind, lit. "life")
is a conspicuous eschatological conception, the *frašōkereti*, or "Regeneration," of which we have said
enough already (p. 72). That the Great Assembly in
such a context should be understood as the concourse
of a Judgement Day seems probable, despite Bartholomae's denial. The plural which here and in
Ys. 31⁴ appears to compromise the sole godhead of
Ahura Mazdâh may fairly be interpreted in the
light of considerations explained above (p. 58): the
"Wise Lords" cannot possibly include any conceptions
outside the circle of the Amesha Spenta, and these
are simply divine attributes together forming a unity.

10. Then indeed shall come upon the Lie the destruction of
delight, but they that get them good name shall be partakers in
the promised reward in the fair abode of Good Thought, of the
Wise One and of Right.

There is abundant choice of renderings for the
word we have given as "delight": tradition took it
as "army," i.e. of the Druj, while Tiele makes it a
proper name, Spayathra, an angel of death, and others
make *skendō spayaθrahyā* "the blow of destruction."
Druj, "the Lie," here means the followers of Druj,
the *dregvatō.*

11. If, O ye mortals, ye mark those commandments that the
Wise One hath ordained, even happiness and pain, the eternal
punishment for the followers of the Lie, and the blessings for the
righteous, then hereafter shall ye have bliss.

The scale on which this book is planned will not
permit a similar full treatment of other Gâthâs; but
what has been attempted will both illustrate the
style of these poems and give some idea of the ambiguities that make it frequently difficult to believe
that two or three versions by first-rate scholars really
all go back to the same original. We have also met
with many of the leading conceptions of Zarathushtra,
expressed in what was clearly intended to be used
as a summary of the creed. The long hymn, *Ys.* 31,
has been represented in Chap. VII. and must not
claim space here. Without further description we
may note *Ys.* 32 as a dialogue, and accordingly beset
with some of the ambiguities we observed in the
second Gâthâ: in some of its stanzas Zarathushtra
is vigorously denouncing the Daēvas. He takes
occasion also to denounce unbelievers of various
kinds. The lines on the sin of Yima we quoted
above (pp. 42 f.). One quotation may be made :—

(*Ys.* 32^{10}) He it is that destroyeth (holy) words, who declares
that the Ox and the Sun are the worst thing to behold with the
eyes, and hath made the pious into followers of the Lie, and
desolateth the pastures and lifteth his weapon against the
righteous.

Bartholomae sees a reference here to nocturnal
orgiastic animal sacrifices perpetrated by the Daēva-
worshippers. We hear more in this hymn of these
enemies of the faith, including even the name of one

family of them, the Grēhmas, who were presumably
foremost among Zarathushtra's antagonists. The
vigorous polemic leaves a vivid impression, for all
its crabbed language. No one could fail to recognise
the outbursts of a real man—unless it might be those
clever people who have recovered the long-lost gift
of recognising Solar Myths in every ancient character
they read of[1]. But this by the way. *Ys.* 33 arrests
us on the threshold with a stanza that may introduce
a conception characteristic of later Parsism. It runs
thus:—

> According as it is with those laws that belong to the former
> [i.e. earthly] life, so shall the Judge act with most just deed
> towards the follower of the Lie and the follower of Right and him
> whose false things and good things balance.

This last word, *hēmemyāsaitē*, is taken by Bartholomae as meaning literally "are mixed (in equal
proportions)": the prefix *hēm* (Skt. *sam*, Greek *á*- in
ἅπαξ, ἄθρους, etc.) suggests the essential element that
is given in the brackets. Roth was the first to recognise in this stanza the later Parsi doctrine of *hamistakân*, as it was called in Pahlavi—a limbo said to
extend from the earth to the stars, in which souls
abide whose record of good and evil is exactly even.
In the Later Avesta it was called *misva gātuš*, "place

---

[1] Drews, in his much-discussed book *Die Christusmythe* (1910),
makes great use of Parsism. He shows his qualification by con-
founding Sraosha and Saoshyant (p. 8 of ed. 4)!

of the mixed," from a kindred adjective. Söderblom,
Mills and Casartelli refuse to believe that the idea is
Gâthic; but the arguments of the last-named scholar
against Roth's translation do not affect Bartholomae's
entirely different reading, which ultimately produces
the same meaning. Even if Bartholomae is wrong in
finding another Gâthic allusion to the Hamistakân
(*Ys.* 48⁴), there seems to be adequate ground for
allowing, with Prof. Williams Jackson, that the stanza
here discussed does foreshadow the doctrine of an
intermediary state, though no doubt the detailed
conception is late. A few minor points of interest
occur in this hymn. The singer speaks of himself
as "I, the priest." Since Zarathushtra is referred
to as "the Judge" in the opening stanza, with the
verb in the third person, it may well be that the
hymn does not profess to come from his hand; and
in any case the *zaotar* is no member of a priestly
caste—that feature is not grafted on the religion till
the coming of the Magi. There are also references
to "Thy Obedience" (*sraoša*)—Mazdâh is addressed
—and to Haurvatât and Ameretât, the Ameshas
Health and Immortality, which enlarge the hitherto
scanty references to these subordinate members of
the celestial hierarchy. The last hymn of this first
Gâthâ, *Ys.* 34, gives us little on which to tarry. We
note a reference to the Saoshyants (p. 53, above), in
which as elsewhere in the Gâthâs the title belongs to

Zarathushtra himself and his foremost helpers, like
Jâmâspa. It has an eschatological connotation, however, by virtue of the fact that these "Deliverers"
are to accomplish the final victory over evil. The
transference of the title to supernatural beings who
are entirely in the future is, as we have seen, post-
Gâthic.

The second Gâthâ, called *uštavaiti*, from its first
word *uštā*, is in a stanza of five equal lines, each
containing $4 + 7$ syllables. This coincides with the
çakvarî Vedic stanza (Arnold, no. 58), an extension of the *trištubh* (cf. Geldner, *Metrik*, p. vii).
It contains four hymns (*Ys.* 43—46), with a total of
66 stanzas, as against 101 in the seven hymns of
Gâthâ Ahunavaiti, which we have just left. The
metre may be represented as before by a literal
translation of one stanza (*Ys.* 43[3]), so as to give the
syllabic value of the lines:—

> May he attain | to what is better than good,
> who would teach us | the straight paths to blessedness
> in this life here | of body and that of thought,
> true paths that lead | to realms where dwells Ahura—
> leal man, like thee, | Mazdâh, well-knowing, holy.

This almost chance-chosen verse will serve to bring
out one or two new features of Gâthic phraseology.
The recurring adjective "like thee" (*θwāvant*) is
always followed by the vocative, "O Mazdâh." Often

it is used of the Prophet himself, as here, where
Zarathushtra, speaking of himself in the third person,
claims that he has likeness to the Deity in that he
is learned in heavenly lore and "holy," or possibly
rather "beneficent" (p. 62): he cherishes the ambition of winning the eternal reward like that promised to the "teachers" in Dan. xii. 2, and those "who
turn many to righteousness." This is another Biblical
verse that would go most naturally into Avestan.
The hymn continues with a recapitulation by the
Prophet of a series of six visions, in which he had
received from Ahura and the Ameshas illumination
on the great themes of his mission. Each opens with
the formula "I recognised Thee as the Holy (or
Beneficent) One, O Wise Lord, when..." The first
of these proceeds "when I saw Thee first at the birth
of Life," that is, the creation of earthly life, as distinguished from the Future Life. Tiele draws from
this verse the inference that for the writer Zarathushtra is a saint of the dim past. This seems
unnecessary, for the assumption that a vision is
being described is altogether simple and reasonable.
The visions successively name the ordaining of the
moral law at the beginning, the divine setting apart
of the Prophet himself and his questioning of Mazdâh
which gave him the revelation, with Vohū Manah
as the constant medium of illumination. There is a
note of urgency which reminds Bartholomae of the

preaching of John, "Repent, for the kingdom of
heaven is at hand": especially note this stanza—

And when thou saidst to me "Thou shalt go to Right to be
instructed," then thou didst not command what I did not obey
"Speed thee, ere my Obedience come, followed by treasure-laden
Recompense, who shall render to men severally the recompense
of the twofold award" (*Ys.* 43¹²).

(Literally "the two blessings," which by an idiom
very common in both branches of Aryan means
"the blessing and the curse.") The visions that
prepared the Prophet for his mission are naturally
followed by the questions in detail addressed by him
to Mazdâh in *Ys.* 44.   The twenty stanzas of the
hymn, except the last (which may be interpolated), all
begin with the recurrent line, unchanged throughout,
"Thus I ask thee, tell me truly, O Lord."   The answer
is in each question to be inferred from the question,
unless this is rather a petition for spiritual blessings
which Ahura may be assumed to give at Zarathushtra's prayer.   The two first stanzas may be roughly
thus rendered :—

This I ask thee—tell me truly, tell me duly, Holy Lord—
How to worship with a service worthy thee, O King adored.
Teach me, Wise One, as the heavenly may the earthly, as to friend
Friend may speak—so may the kindly Right his timely succour
    bring,
And with heaven's Good Thought to usward in his gracious power
    descend.

Tell me duly, tell me truly as I pray, O Holy King:
When the Highest Life is dawning, at thy Kingdom's opening,
Shall the dooms of heaven's tribunal give to every man his due?
Surely he, the holy prophet, to his watchful soul doth lay
All men's sin, yet ever friendly doth the worlds of life renew.

The stanzas that follow have been already cited
(p. 86). The rest of the questions largely concern
the rewards and punishments that are to follow
orthodox and heretic, mostly in the future life. But
the poet is not so engrossed with the other world as
to ignore the present. We have already seen how
practical Zarathushtra is, and how convinced he is
that industry as a farmer makes up a large proportion
of the whole duty of man. It is therefore quite con-
gruous when he asks the rather grotesque-sounding
question,

Shall I indeed, O thou the Right, obtain that reward, even ten
mares with a stallion and a camel, which was promised to me,
O Wise One, even as through thee the future gift of Health and
Immortality? (Ys. 44[18]).

We need not judge severely the determination to
make the best of both worlds, nor the intolerance
which animates the Prophet as he claims the future
blessedness for himself and his followers, fiercely
invoking divine judgement upon the foes of his faith
and (it would seem) rival prophets who strove to
pervert what he felt to be the right ways of Ahura.
The days were not yet born when a reformer of

profound convictions would account it less than
virtue to say

I was ordained at the first by thee : all other I look upon with
hatred of the soul (*Ys.* 44^{11}).

The next hymn (*Ys.* 45) invites fuller treatment,
as it is of great importance for the theology of the
reform : we may translate it entire, relying this time
largely on Geldner (in *Grundriss,* II. 30) as well as
Bartholomae.

1. I will speak forth : hear now and hearken now, ye who from
near desire (instruction), ye who from far. Now observe him
[i.e. Ahura ?] in your mind, all of you, for he is manifested. Never
shall the false teacher destroy the Second Life, the follower of the
Lie, who with his tongue perverted (men) to evil beliefs.

2. I will speak of the twain spirits at the beginning of the
world, of whom the holier thus addressed the fiendly one :
"Neither our thoughts, nor our teachings, nor our wills, nor our
beliefs, nor our words, nor our deeds, nor our selves, nor our souls
can be in harmony."

3. I will speak of that which the Wise Lord the all-knowing
revealed to me in the beginning of this (earthly) life. Those of
you that put not in practice this word as I think and utter it, to
them shall be woe at the end of life.

4. I will speak of that is best in this life—from Right the
Wise One knoweth it, who created the same, even the father of
the active Good Thought [i.e. the doctrine of Agriculture]; and the
daughter of the same is Aramaiti of goodly deeds. Not to be
deceived is the all-seeing Lord.

Both Geldner and Bartholomae render " I have learnt
it, O Mazdâh," which seems to involve a change of

text. The true faith of Agriculture is apparently the "father" of Good Thought, which is here really collective, the pious workers in the field. Another Amesha, the genius of the Earth (p. 63), is also child of this "greatest thing in the world," which the all-knowing Mazdâh knows through Asha, the Right Order of things, essentially a part of his own self.

5. I will speak of that which the Holiest declared unto me as the word that is best for mortals' hearing: he, the Wise Lord (said), "They who at my bidding render to him [i.e. Zarathushtra] obedience, they all shall attain unto Health and Immortality by the deeds of the Good Spirit."

6. I will speak of what is best of all, praising him, O thou the Right, who is bounteous to all that live. By his holy spirit may the Wise Lord hear, in whose praise I have been taught by Good Thought. By his wisdom let him teach me what is best.

7. He whose two awards [cf. p. 102] as he disposeth all living men shall receive [or, less probably, "whose blessings all living men should desire"], and they that have been and they that shall be. In immortality shall the soul of the righteous be joyful: in eternity shall be the torments on the men that follow the Lie. And all this the Wise Lord doth appoint by his Dominion.

8. Him thou shouldst seek to win for us by praises of worship, for now have I seen it with mine eye, that which is of the Good Spirit and of (good) deed and word, knowing by the Right the Wise Lord: so will we offer him homage in the House of Song.

9. Him thou shouldst seek to propitiate for us with Good Thought, who at his will maketh us weal or woe. May the Wise Lord by his Dominion bring us to work, that we may prosper our beasts and our men, for our assurance of Good Thought gained through the Right.

10. Him thou shouldst honour with the prayers of Devotion (Aramaiti), him that is called Wise Lord for ever, for that he hath promised through his Rightness and Good Thought Health and Immortality to be in his Dominion, strength and continuance in his house.

11. Whoso therefore in the future lightly esteemeth the Daēvas and those mortals who lightly esteem him [i.e. Saošyant], even all others save that one who highly esteemeth him,—unto him shall the holy Self of the Deliverer (Saošyant) as Lord of the house be friend, brother or father, O Thou Wise Lord.

The last two stanzas here have some points of special interest. In the tenth we note that all six Ameshas are named, and linked by the possessive pronoun with Mazdâh. In the eleventh we are again in the eschatological realm: Zarathushtra is promising to stand by his faithful followers in the Judgement— they shall be to him then as his own personal friend, brother or even father. There is nothing here to exclude Zarathushtra's authorship, for he speaks as a Prophet in profound conviction that the truth he brings will save at the last. We are reminded how in *Ys.* 46[10] he promises to cross with them the "Bridge of the Separater" (p. 71). The lofty tone of this great seer is best realised when we compare the eschatology of the Fourth Gospel. There are indeed other striking parallels here; for the Prophet calls himself not only "Saviour" but "Lord of the house" (*dēng pati*, identical with δεσπότης), thus re-calling Matt. xiii. 27 and xx. 1 (and x. 25 !) in a context

curiously like Mark iii. 35. But the Parsi traditional
rendering spoils this : a theory of dependence would
require that the Gâthâs were better understood in
Palestine than in Persia.

Last in this Gâthâ comes *Ys.* 46, a hymn of the
persecuted. It has nineteen stanzas, falling into
sections but loosely bound together ; and this, com-
bined with the obviously corrupt state of the text
in sundry places, suggests that the unity of the poem
is not beyond question. The poem starts with an
almost despairing cry—

1. To what land shall I go to flee, whither to flee ? From
nobles and my peers they sever me, nor are the people pleased
with me [...a corruption in text...], nor the rulers of the land that
follow the Lie : how am I to please thee, O thou Wise Lord ?

2. I know wherefore I am without success, O Wise One :
(because) few cattle are mine, and for that I have but few folk.
I cry to thee ; see thou to it, Lord, granting me support, as
friend giveth to friend. Teach me by the Right the acquisition
of Good Thought [i.e. Paradise].

These stanzas, and others like them telling of savage
raids upon quiet pastoral people, only desirous of
security in avocations sacred to Ahura and beneficial
to men, belong obviously to a period or a district in
which the religion had as yet won no firm hold. The
speaker may well be Zarathushtra himself, who would
thus appear to have originally practised the agri-
cultural life which he preached as the ideal. It is
hard to reconcile this situation with that of a later

section in this hymn, where Zarathushtra recounts
to Ahura the names of his leading adherents, including King Vîshtâspa and the other men of high degree
who followed him in the days of his triumph. We
may safely assume that fragments have been unskil-
fully pieced together, though their authenticity as
separate items need not be questioned.

We pass to the Third Gâthâ, called *Spentā-mainyū*
from its first two words. The stanza is composed of
four lines with 4 + 7 syllables, thus agreeing with the
metre of the Second except in its containing one line
less. There are four hymns in the Gâthâ, consisting
severally of six, twelve, twelve and eleven stanzas.
Ys. 47 is as featureless as it is short. We may as
before give the opening verse in the metre of the
original, which will enable the reader again to notice
how in a poem designed for worship the six Ameshas
are once more gathered all together under the head-
ship of Ahura.

> By his blest Spirit | and by the Best Thought
> and deed and word | according unto the Right
> The Wise joined with | Dominion and Devotion
> shall give to us | Health and Immortality.

The stanza is almost a mnemonic, into which is also
ingeniously woven the fundamental triad of Thought,
Word and Deed, as an expansion of Vohū Manah.
The triad is suggested again in the next stanza by
mention of tongue, hands and intellect; while four

Ameshas are worked in, and Mazdâh is declared to
be the father of Asha, Truth or Rightness, the Good
Order, as in the next verse he is of the Holy Spirit
(*spenta mainyu*)—in this context mostly the spirit
of a pious man, though the distinction is as hard to
draw as it is sometimes in the New Testament. We
have in this short hymn a maximum of characteristic
terms brought in, almost suggesting that it was a
neophyte's first lesson. There is the Ox, and the
Fire by which the followers of Asha and of Druj
shall at last be parted, and the demon world represented by Aka Manah, Ill Thought, as well as by the
older Druj. *Ys.* 48 is not such a bundle of dry bones,
though a bundle it is, of rather disconnected snatches
which may well have no original unity. The first
part is eschatological, with one stanza which Bartholomae and Geldner very plausibly set by *Ys.* 33[1]
as a reference to the Hamistakân (pp. 98 f.):—

Whoso, O Wise One, maketh his thought better and (then)
worse, and (likewise) his Self by deed and word, and followeth his
own inclinations, wishes and choices, he shall according to thy will
be separated at the last (*Ys.* 48[4]).

The hymn ends with three stanzas which Bartholomae
acutely interprets as an appeal to the still uncon-
verted class of the nobles—*narō*, which may mean
simply "men," but like its cognate ἀνήρ and the
Latin cognomen *Nero* (with Umbrian *nerf*, "chiefs")
may be specialised to denote an upper class.

When, O Wise One, will the nobles understand the Message ? When wilt thou smite the pollution of this intoxicant, through which the Karapans [p. 69] evilly deceive, and the wicked lords of the lands with purpose fell ? (*Ys.* 48^{10}).

Bartholomae finds here the old Haoma, the Indian Soma that reappeared in the Yashts. Alcohol was indeed a product of prehistoric Indo-European barbarism, for the *mada* of this passage is first cousin to the Greek $\mu\acute{\epsilon}\theta\upsilon$ and the English *mead*. Passing on to *Ys.* 49, we find ourselves in the immediate presence of the most urgent difficulties of the early propaganda. A certain Bēndva, apparently a chief who fosters *daēva*-worship, is fiercely denounced as the worst hindrance to the Prophet's work. His deeds of rapine and teachings of falsehood are attacked, and contrasted with the loyalty of Frashaoshtra and Jâmâspa. A comprehensive curse at the end paints the ultimate future of these rebels :—

But these that are of an evil dominion, of evil deeds, evil words, evil self and evil thought, followers of the Lie, the Souls go to receive them with foul food : in the House of the Lie shall they be meet inhabitants (*Ys.* 49^{11}).

The Gâthâ is closed with *Ys.* 50, a homogeneous composition after the first three verses. As in the other hymns of this part of the Parsi Psalter, the imprecatory element is to the front; but it soon fades into a fervent prayer for the future reward of the faithful Prophet and his community. One striking

stanza we came near giving earlier (p. 86), in our
small collection of passages where the seer's earnest-
ness allows him to deviate into poetry.

The Fourth and Fifth Gâthâs consist of only one
hymn apiece. *Ys.* 51, called *Gāθā Vohūχšaθrā* from
its first words, has twenty-two stanzas containing
three lines with 7 + 7 syllables. The metre may
again be represented with a specimen:—

The good Desired Dominion, | a most surpassing portion,
even this shall Right accomplish | for him that by deeds with zeal
achieves the Best, O Wise One. | That will I now win for us.

The hymn presents us with little that is artistically
noteworthy, but we may quote a stanza which crystal-
lises the doctrine of retribution very clearly :—

The Wise Lord who through his Dominion gives what is
better than good to him that is attentive to his will, but what is
worse than evil to him that obeyeth him not, at the latter end of
life (*Ys.* 51[6]).

The outward circumstance of Judgement is seen in
another verse:—

What joy through thy two ministers [so Williams Jackson—
Bartholomae gives "What as reward to the two sides," i.e. good
and bad] thou wilt give, O Mazdâh, to the destruction of the
wicked but to save the righteous, a sign (of that) give us for our
souls (*Ys.* 51[9]—Prof. Jackson's version).

The prospect of final damnation for those who reject
the truth fills the thought of the seer up to the end,

together with the assurance of bliss for his faithful
friends. We may quote one curious verse which
Bartholomae, in a weighty compressed note on Zarathushtra's historical reality (*Altiran. Wörterb.* 1675),
selects as "significant for the reality of the conditions
under which the Gâthâs arose ":—

> The Kavi's wanton did not please Zarathushtra Spitama at the
> Winter Gate, in that he stayed him from taking refuge with him,
> and when there came to him also (Zarathushtra's) two steeds
> shivering with cold (*Ys.* 51¹²).

Zarathushtra is overtaken by a storm, when travelling in the bitter cold of a Persian winter, and is
repulsed by the servant of Bēndva (?), a *Kavi*, or
chief, of the old *daēva*-worshipping clans : he fiercely
calls him by an opprobrious name. The stanza certainly presents difficulties to the would-be allegoriser ;
and the believer in the legendary character of the
central figure of the Gâthâs will find it hard to
discover a meaning for a palpable incident of real
life.

Last we come to the *Gāθā Vahištō-išti*, consisting
of *Ys.* 53. The metre is rather complex—four lines with
$7 + 5, 7 + 5, 7 + 7 + 5, 7 + 7 + 5$ syllables respectively.
It is a marriage hymn, celebrating the nuptials of
the Prophet's youngest daughter Pouruchistâ with
Jâmâspa, whom we have met before. Though the
hymn is corrupt and very difficult, it may be as well
to give a provisional translation of it, adopting

mostly Bartholomae's interpretation with a general caveat as to the possibility of very different views— as may be seen, for instance, by anyone who consults Professor Mills in *Sacred Books of the East* (XXXI.). We must not pause for any discussion.

1. *Zarathushtra.* The best possession known is that of Zarathushtra Spitama, which is that the Wise Lord will grant to him through the Right the glories of blessed life unto all time. (So is it) also for them who practise and learn the words and works of his Good Religion.

2. Then let them seek the pleasure of the Wise One with thought, words and actions gladly unto his praise, and (seek) his worship, even the Kavi Vîshtâspa, and Zarathushtra's son the Spitamid [Ishatvâstra by name], and Frashaoshtra, making straight the paths for the Religion of the Deliverer [Saoshyant] which the Lord appointed.

3. Him, O Pouruchistâ, thou scion of Haēcathaspa and Spitama, youngest of Zarathushtra's daughters, hath he [the Prophet] appointed as one to enjoin upon thee the fellowship with Good Thought, Rightness and the Wise One. So take counsel with thine own understanding : with good insight practise the holiest works of Devotion [Aramaiti].

4. *Jâmâspa.* Earnestly will I lead her to the Faith, that she may serve her father and her husband, the farmers and the nobles, as a righteous woman (serving) the righteous. The glorious heritage of Good Thought […(three syllables corrupt)] shall the Wise Lord grant to her good Self for all time.

5. *Zarathushtra.* Teachings address I to maidens marrying and to you [bridegrooms], giving counsel. Lay them to heart, and learn to get them within your own Selves in earnest attention to the life of Good Thought. Let each of you seek to excel the other in the Right, for it will be a prize for that one.

6. So is it in fact, ye men and women ! Whatever fortune ye look for in union with the Lie [...(corrupt)]. To them, the followers of the Lie, crying Woe !, shall be ill food ; happiness shall flee away from those that injure righteousness. In such wise do ye destroy for yourselves the spiritual life.

7. And there shall be for you the reward of this community, if most faithful zeal be with the wedded pair (?), where in the abyss the spirit of the follower of the Lie, shrinking and cowering, shall fall into perdition. Separate ye from the Community, so shall your word at the last be Woe !

8. So they whose deeds are evil, let them be the deceived, and they that are reprobate let them cry out all of them. By good rulers let him give slaughter and bloodshed to them, and peace for the happy homedwellers. Grief let him bring on those, he that is greatest, with the chain of death ; and soon let it be !

9. To them of evil belief belongs the place of corruption. They that go to despise the worthy, contemners of Right, who forfeit their own self—where is the righteous Lord that shall rob them of life and freedom ? Thine, Wise One, is the Dominion, whereby thou canst give to the right-living poor the better portion.

Rather a sombre marriage song !

Before we leave the Gâthâs we must give the three great Prayers, which take a supreme place in the ritual. It is not at first sight easy to see why they take such precedence : like the " Gâyatrī " of the Rigveda, they hardly seem adequate for so much emphasis, from the standpoint of the religion to which they minister. But the reader may judge. First comes the *Ahuna Vairya* or *Honover* (*Ys.* 27¹³), in a metre form containing three lines with $7+9$ syllables apiece. It may be thus rendered after Bartholomae :—

Even as he (Zarathushtra) is the Lord (*ahū*, whence *Ahura*) for us to choose, so is he the Judge, according to Rightness, he that bringeth the life-works of Good Thought unto the Wise One, and (so) the Dominion unto the Lord, even he whom they made shepherd for the poor.

This prayer, or rather creed, was intelligible in the early period, but the key must have been lost before long : a glance at other versions, such as Tiele's (*Geschichte der Religion*, II. 186), will sufficiently show how unrecognisable the stanza may easily be made. The version we have adopted is supported not only by the authority of Bartholomae, but also in the main by that of Geldner, who rendered it on these lines generally in his *Studien* (1882, pp. 144 ff.). It becomes essentially eschatological. The Prophet is marked out by Asha, the Right Order of things, to take command of this life, and then at the last to present before God the life-works of his faithful followers : Vohū Manah, as so often, has a practically collective significance. This final work will cause the Kingdom of God to come, the complete victory over the forces of Evil. From the last function of the Prophet the verse comes back to his preparatory work in this life, where he is " shepherd of the poor," the oppressed agriculturists whose toil is pleasing to

Ahura, but harried perpetually by the fierce nomads who follow the ancient gods. This interpretation of a very dark saying may not be certain, but it gives the words an adequate meaning, and accounts for their preeminent sanctity.

Next comes the *Ašem vohū* (*Ys.* 27[14]), which on Bartholomae's interpretation is a play upon two meanings of Asha (p. 61). Primarily denoting abstract Right, the divine order, it comes to mean (2) right-doing, action in accord with Right, and (3) a man's rights, as determined by that divine order. This enigmatic sentence, which Geldner gives as prose (*Grundriss*, II. 27), but Bartholomae as three lines with 7, 9 and 3 + 5 syllables, runs thus :—

> Right is the best good : it falls by desire, it falls by desire
> to our portion, even our right to that which is the best right.

He who lives rightly gets his rights in the end, and therefore

> because right is right, to follow right
> Were wisdom in the scorn of consequence.

More complex is the *Airyēmā išyō* (*Ys.* 54[1]), which seems to be in the metre of the last Gâthâ (Geldner): Bartholomae prints it in six lines of 4 + 7, 4 + 7, 3 + 5, 4 + 7, 4 + 7, 3 + 5 syllables respectively—a metre recalling two or three Vedic systems

(Arnold, p. 246, nos. 36, 39, 40). We may tentatively render :—

Let the dear Healer (?) come for support of Zarathushtra's men and women, for support of Good Thought. Whatever Self may win the precious meed of Right, I entreat of this the dear reward that the Wise Lord bestowed (?).

Airyēman, doubtfully rendered Healer on the strength of definitions in the Vendîdâd, is a figure of Aryan antiquity, for Aryamán is the name of an Âditya or archangel in Indian lore. He appears in the Gâthâs elsewhere only in the word *airyēman*, meaning "comrade," a term apparently of rank, attaching to a priestly order : so at least says Bartholomae. Are we to assign this prayer to the period of the "Gâthâ of Seven Chapters" (p. 74), dating from the post-Zarathushtrian epoch in which so many of the old Iranian gods came back to their own again ?

Last comes the *yēṅhē̄ hātam* (*Ys.* 27[15]), a little fragment of three lines with 4 + 7 syllables each— the metre called in Sanskrit *virâj*, or *tripadâ triṣṭubh* (Arnold, no. 16). It is not in Gâthic dialect but in Later Avestan, though it is of course possible that it has been transferred by adaptation. However that may be, we had better treat it here. Geldner observes that it is an imitation of the last stanza of the Fourth Gâthâ (*Ys.* 51[22]) : it seems quite possible that it was derived from it by simply paring down the fourteen-

syllable lines so as to fit a more familiar metre.
That makes its post-Gâthic date fairly certain. It
may be rendered thus :—

The man among all that are, the women too, to whom for his
prayer (*yasna*) the Wise Lord knows the better portion doth fall,
in accordance with Right, these men and women do we reverence.

We may put beside this its model :—

He, I ween, that, among all that have been and are, the Wise
Lord knoweth as one to whom in accordance with Right the best
portion falls for his prayer, these will I reverence by their names,
and go before them with honour (*Ys.* 51²²).

Here the summary follows a glowing eulogy of the
leading men whose help has at last prospered Zarathushtra's mission. It is somewhat suspicious that
here only in the Gâthâs is the verb *yaz* (whence
Yasna and *Yasht*—the Greek ἅζομαι and ἅγιος)
applied to men : the possibility may be admitted
that the Gâthâ has been rounded off with a stanza
in the style of later worship, which was quite
addicted to "worship" of the *fravashi* (pp. 141 ff.)
of a living man.

CHAPTER IX

THE YASHTS AND LATER AVESTA

THE step from Gâthâs into Yashts is a step into a new world. The dialect is different, but this has little to do with the sensation of strangeness that comes over us, for the difference is not greater than we note when we move from one English county to another two or three hundred miles away. We still meet the old familiar names : Ahura Mazdâh is still supreme, with the Amesha Spentas around him, and Zarathushtra is still the Prophet of the Faith. But even while we shut our eyes to the new divine names which crowd upon us, we cannot help seeing that the familiar names carry new associations. The Prophet is no longer a man of like passions with ourselves, a fervid religious and moral Reformer, eagerly pressing his lofty doctrine of God and duty against much opposition, and exhibiting very human emotions of elation and discouragement as the fortunes of the

campaign sway to and fro. He is a purely supernatural figure, holding converse with Ahura Mazdâh
on theological and ritual subjects, which rarely come
near the practical and homely religion inculcated by
the singer of the Gâthâs.   Nor is Ahura himself less
changed.   He is nominal head of a hierarchy in
which we soon find old gods in what are virtually old
relationships : if they are *pro forma* subordinated as
angels, they do not get less worship.   Sacrifice on a
large scale becomes the centre of religion, and we
realise by the contrast how strangely absent the
institution has been in our reading of the Gâthâs.
Prayer has mostly degenerated into spells, in which
the use of the right title for deity takes the prominence we know so well when we read magical texts
or the hymns of ritual religion.   In other words, we
are back again in the pre-Reformation days.   The
authors of the Yashts are first cousins to those of
the Veda.   They have learnt nothing since the days
of Aryan unity, except some new gods to set in
their pantheon, and forgotten extremely little.   Had
Zarathushtra come back awhile from the House of
Song, he would have had to begin his work over
again ; nor would he have abated his censure of this
new *daēvayasna* because his own name had become
semi-divine.

The limits of our subject do not allow us to show
how far this lost ground was regained in the revival

of religion under the Sassanian kings ; nor need we stay longer to recapitulate what has been already sketched above (Chap. VI.). If the contrast between Gâthâs and Yashts is violent on the side of religion, it is scarcely less conspicuous from the literary point of view. The difference of metrical form has been already described, and we have seen how the uniform metre of the verse in the Yashts agrees with that which gains increasing predominance in India from the Vedic period onwards—an outward and visible sign of that close kinship with the other branch of the Aryan family which we have seen interrupted by the Zarathushtrian Reform. But this external difference is a small part of the contrast. The crabbed, compressed, obscure style of the Gâthâs has been replaced by language which is generally easy and clear enough, though its lucidity is very largely the effect of a great poverty of ideas. Formulae are ubiquitous, and repetitions perpetual. A favourite form in the glorification of successive *Yazatas* is the piling up of epithets for some lines together. Such strings of adjectives may in skilful hands produce a striking literary effect : one recalls a superb passage in the *Wisdom of Solomon* (vii. 22 f.), and familiar sentences in the artless prose of Paul. But the poets of the Yashts are generally artificial rather than artistic; and if they become simple, they are not so much artless as bald, through the absence of the intensity which makes the simplest language glow. This general verdict needs qualifying with one or two counter-statements. As might be expected where the work of many different hands is gathered into one book, there are very varying degrees of literary merit ; and in one instance, as we shall see, a nameless author has achieved a supremely beautiful conception, or inherited it and given it expression. Then we should also observe that for all their wearisome repetitions the Yashts are not dull, if we know how to skip. There is abundance of curious lore, folk-legend, and epic material in embryo, such as finds full expression centuries later in the *Shâh-nâmeh.* For matter of this kind we shall stop as we go through the Yashts, always assuming that verse form brings it within the limits of our subject. But where these elements are missing we may perhaps excuse our silence by pleading that our title only makes room for "poetry," and by inference allows us to ignore mere verse when we are so inclined.

Professor Geldner, in his concise account of Avestan literature in the second volume of the Iranian *Grundriss,* makes an important distinction between the Yashts in our collection in the matter of their form. A true Yasht has a division into cantos with a fixed introduction and a refrain. Thus many Yashts contain a succession of heroes (or

others) who worshipped the Yazata, asked a boon
and got it (or failed). This will be described in set
formulae, with no variation in introduction or refrain
except for the name of the new worshipper. On this
test Geldner rejects all the Yashts but eleven, viz.
nos. 5, 8, 9, 10, 13, 14, 15, 16, 17, 19 and the Srôsh
Yasht (*Ys.* 57). It will be seen that this test rules
out also Yashts which we shall pass by on the ground
of their preponderance of prose. On this subject we
have said enough in Chap. III. We have seen that
the Yashts were interpolated with prose when still
only deutero-canonical, like Daniel and Esther when
the Greek version was made. Many of the Yashts
bear obvious signs of dislocated text : sections have
been torn away, and sections of alien origin brought
into a context that does not suit them. With this
naturally goes considerable corruption in the text
of individual passages. The history of the Avesta, as
sketched above (pp. 13 ff.), is sufficient explanation
of these derangements : we can only wonder that
they are not more serious still.

With this preface we may proceed to review the
Yashts. There is hardly anything in the first four
of them, which are largely in prose, and ill preserved, late and uninteresting to boot. *Yt.* 1 stands
at the head as addressed to Ahura, whose appropriate titles are enumerated. A verse spell without
original connexion may be cited as a sample :

we attempt a verse rendering in confidence that
we cannot fall below the level of the poetry we
translate :—

> By the holy Aramaiti
> All their malice break to pieces,
> Bind their hands and tear their ears off,
> Maim their knees [*v.l.* weapons] and bind in fetters (?) (*Yt.* 1²⁷).

The citing of this elegant extract will serve as an
adequate reason for making no further efforts in this
line.   A solitary fragment of verse in the third Yasht
(dedicated to Asha Vahishta) may be cited for special
reasons :—

> Headlong down from heaven fell he,
> He of demons the most lying,
> Angra Mainyu many-slaying (*Yt.* 3¹³).

The word rendered *heaven* here (*dyaoš*—ablative of
dyāuš) is interesting as the only survival in the
Avesta of the primitive Indo-European word *dyēus,
sky,* for which see above, p. 33.   The Fiend falling
from the sky belongs to old folklore about war in
heaven between powers of light and darkness : we
are very familiar with the application of a similar
idea in the Revelation.

The fourth Yasht, named from Haurvatât, the
Amesha " Health " or " Well-being," is specially corrupt, and its verse-snatches are only spells.   With
the fifth we come at last to coherent and ancient

material. The Yasht is in honour of the river genius
Ardvi Sûra Anâhita, partly as representative of
the Waters, of which she was the queen. It will
be remembered that the Waters were among the
highest objects of reverence in the Persian religion
described by Herodotus (pp. 35 and 38 above).
Suggestions as to the earlier history of the name
Anâhita, well known to the Greeks as Anaïtis, were
given above : we need only reinforce them here
by remarking that if our extant Yashts can enable
us by their relative length, integrity and apparent
antiquity to estimate the importance of the deities
worshipped in the community that produced these
hymns, we can find no rival but Mithra, her partner
in Herodotus (seemingly) and on the highly significant
Hamadan inscription of Artaxerxes Mnemon, who
joins them with Auramazda as a trinity. Next to
them on this test would come Tishtrya (*Yt.* 8),
Drvâspa (*Yt.* 9), the Fravashis (*Yt.* 13), Verethraghna
(*Yt.* 14), Vayu (*Yt.* 15), Ashi (*Yt.* 17), the Hvarenō
(*Yt.* 19), and Haoma (*Ys.* 9). None of these is even
named in the Gâthâs : the deities of this period form
a wholly independent pantheon, in which Ahura
Mazdâh and the Amesha Spentas are almost
strangers. The part taken by Ahura in Yasht 5 is
worth a little attention. He is only named about
ten times in the verse parts of the Yasht, generally as Creator. Thus the earth is " Ahura-made "

(l. [88]), so is Victory (l. [86]); Anâhita comes "from the Creator Mazdâh" (l. [7]), who has "made four steeds" for her (l. [120]). Just as he has "made thee judge of the corporeal world," says Anâhita to Zarathushtra, so "hath he made me"...what the verse fails to say—the prose goes on "protectress of all the world of good." This agrees with the familiar formula of the Persian Kings at Persepolis and Nakš-i-Rustam :—

A great god is Auramazda, who created this earth, who created yon heaven, who created man, who created welfare for man, who made Darius [etc.] king, one king of many, one lord of many.

Such declarations regularise the doctrine, and make the supremacy of Ahura clear. If the Yashts represent a phase of the religion which prevailed for a time in some outlying part of the empire of the Achaemenid Kings, we can understand this degree of conformity to the court worship of Auramazda, and at the same time realise the patent fact that the old Aryan nature-gods loomed much larger than he in the real thoughts of priests who sang these hymns. This consideration will explain an otherwise astonishing stanza which opens the long list of Anâhita's worshippers that extends over about half the Yasht. We attempt to reproduce the mixture of verse and prose which presumably must guide us in our effort to trace its original form.

Her worshipped
  Ahura Mazdâh, Creator
in the *Airyana Vaējah* [home-land of Iran—locality unknown],
on the goodly Daitya (river) ;
  Came with milk and Hôm, with barsom,
  Came with skill of tongue, with Manthra,
with word and act and libations and right-spoken utterances.
Then he prayed of her,
  Upon me bestow this blessing,
thou good, beneficent Ardvi Sûra Anâhita,
  That the son of Pourushaspa,
  Him the righteous Zarathushtra,
  I may lead to thinking, speaking,
  Acting after my Religion.
Ardvi Sûra Anâhita bestowed on him this blessing, even on
him as he at once brought libations, devoutly worshipped and
prayed, bestowing the blessing (*Yt.* 5^{17-19}).

(A word of commentary is needed before we go
on. For Hôm, or Haoma, see p. 41. *Manθra* is a
spell. The barsom (*baresman*) is a Magian ritual
instrument, a bundle of twigs held before the face :
cf. Ezekiel viii. 17. It adapts the name of an Aryan
institution of a very different kind, the Indian *barhis*,
or carpet of grass on which the sacrifice was laid.)

The passage thus printed—a fair sample of a
phenomenon perpetually recurrent in the Yashts—
forms an easy exercise in higher criticism. We find
later on (ll. [104-106]) that Zarathushtra also sacrificed to
Anâhita in the Iranian home-land, and that he offered
the same ritual gift, one very characteristic of fully
developed Parsism, in contrast to the other heroes,

who all come with a hundred horses (like the Indian
açvamedha, familiar to us from Southey's *Curse of
Kehama*), a thousand bulls and ten thousand sheep.
His prayer is in identic language, with the sub-
stitution of Kavi Vîshtâspa, his Constantine, for his
own name. It is easy to see that the second section
is original and the first modelled upon it when
Anâhita was to be credited with the first impulse
by which Zarathushtra himself became the prophet
of the Religion; unless indeed both alike merely
apply with new names inserted the verse formula
in which any priest's ritual was described. The
accretion of prose glosses is here very obvious, and
typical of the Yashts as a whole.

Space forbids a lengthened description of this
interesting Yasht. Its concluding section may be
referred to first, as it affects the whole character
of a goddess of supreme importance in this stage
of Persian religion. We find here a description
of Anâhita, in verse throughout, and extraordinarily
full of pictorial detail. Windischmann can hardly
be wrong in tracing it to typical statues of the goddess. If that is so, we are tempted at once to
compare the descriptions of the Ephesian "Great
Artemis," who was in any case first cousin to
Anâhita: we may note that the chief priest at
Ephesus bore a Persian title, Μεγάβυζος, *baga-
buχša*, "delivered by the deity." Sir W. M. Ramsay
(in Hastings' *Bible Dictionary* I. 605) describes the

Ephesian so-called Artemis fully from coins and statues, and we may select two features for comparison. In the first place, "the upper part of the body in front is covered with rows of breasts, symbolising her function as the nourishing mother of all life." With this we compare the Yasht (l. [127]) :—

> Tightened she her cincture, making
> Shapely breasts and full of beauty.

The latter looks as if civilised art had been at work upon the barbaric figure which Ephesus was not Hellenised enough to improve upon. Our Persian sculptor's Anâhita is completely human, but she keeps the attributes which were symbolised by the shapeless block with the many-breasted bust above : the Yasht repeatedly tells us how maidens besought her for husbands and young wives for happy childbirth. We are further told that Artemis' "head is surmounted either by a lofty ornament, *polos*, or by a mural crown, and something like a heavy veil hangs on each side of the face down to the shoulders." Without laying stress on the "costly mantle" Anâhita wears (l. [126]), we may perhaps trace resemblance in the headdress :—

> Bound she diadem upon her,
> Hundred-starred it was and golden,
> Doubly quartered, wheel-shaped, splendid,
> Streamer-decked, full-spreading, shapely (l. [128]).

Though painfully conscious of trespassing on the

preserves of archaeologists and historians of art,
we venture to recognise here a definite artistic
development which prompts inferences as to the
culture attained by the people among whom the
Yashts first gained currency.   We leave the hint
to the specialists for what it is worth, candidly
warning them however that much may turn on the
right interpretation of some questionable words in
the Avestan extracts given.

We must not tarry much longer, and will only
add one or two notes on items in what we have
called the epic material of the Yasht.   We are told
of the *paradāta*, heroes of a primeval age, standing
to Mazdeism rather like Noah and Abraham to
Mosaism, who worshipped Anâhita and won their
sovranty through her.   Sometimes by way of variety
the arch-enemies of these patriarchs appeal to Anâhita in the same formula, and the sequel is told in
the invariable form, but with the laconic negative
added.   One of these foes is Azhi Dahâka, a *daēva*-
worshipping king of Iran, conceived as a three-headed
serpent.   It is very noteworthy that the locality of
his invocation is Babylon, indicating apparently an
early feud between Aryan and Chaldaean.   We must
close our sketch of the Yasht by quoting one section,
obviously prepared for the first Parsi aviator.   The
prose interpolation is significant[1].

[1] Some lines where the metre shows corruption are obelised.   The
extract opens with a twelve-syllabled verse : see p. 18.

[61] Her worshipped
 Paurva once, the skilful sailor,
 When the conquering, strong Thraētaona[1]
 Whirled him vulture-formed to heaven.
[62] Full three days on flew he homewards,
 Three nights, yet descend he could not.
 †Three nights past, he came to morning,
 To the shining of the Mighty[2];
 Cried he out to Ardvi Sûra:
[63] O Anâhita, speed hither,
 Swiftly bring me thy protection.
A thousand libations will I bring, mixed with Hôm and milk,
piously prepared, strained, by the Rangha [Tigris] river,
 If alive I win to earthward,
 Earth of Ahura's creation,
 To the home that is my dwelling.
[64] †Hastened Ardvi Sûra to him,
 As a maiden fair and lusty,
 Tall, high-cinctured, stately, noble—
 Lineage hers of great possessions.
 †Shod with buskins ankle-reaching
 Came she, golden-pointed (?), shining.
[65] On his arms her firm grasp laid she—
 Swift her aid and did not tarry—
 That he won with rapid gliding
 Earth of Ahura's creation,
 To the home that was his dwelling,
 Safe and sound, unharmed as ever.

---

[1] Ferîdûn of the Shâhnâmeh. The boatman had apparently tried to dispute the hero's passage of the Tigris, and Thraetaona turned him into a vulture.

[2] Probably the Dawn, but there is deep-seated corruption here.

Past the short prose Yashts addressed to the Sun
and the Moon, we come to the hymn to Tishtrya,
which is probably the star Sirius[1] (*Yt.* 8). It is
about half the length of that we have just left, and
the verse form is preserved fairly well as far as l. 47.
Tishtrya is the chief of the four great stars named in
the Avesta, all of them (as is natural) appearing in
this Yasht. They guard four quarters of the sky,
and have been conjecturally identified as Fomalhaut (Satavaēsa) for the S.W., Vega (Vanant) for
N.W., and the Great Bear (Haptō-iringa) for N.E.,
the stars being roughly in these quarters when
Sirius rises first before the sun in the S.E.[2] Each of

[1] If we may venture on etymological conjecture, Σείριος may be
"Twinkler," from a root *tveis*; and this looks like a doublet of *teis*,
from which *Tištrya* comes naturally. But of course we cannot argue
the point here.

[2] On this point, where the authorities differ considerably, and
there is no evidence how far the opinions expressed are supported by
experts in a field very far away from that of the Zendist, I have
thought it well to consult my friend the Rev. R. Killip, F.R.A.S., who
has kindly secured for me a further opinion from Mr E. W. Maunder
of Greenwich Observatory. Mr Maunder, assuming the latitude 38° N.
(about that of Merv) and the epoch 400 B.C., says that at the moment
of Sirius' rising (E.S.E.), Fomalhaut was setting (S.W. by S.), Vega
being 18° high (N.W. by W.) and the Great Bear wholly visible, with
η on the meridian, sub-polar. "Reviewing the whole problem, the
most *symmetrical* solution would obviously be to take the four as
Sirius, Fomalhaut, Vega and Charles' Wain. All four would be close
to the horizon, and would be 90° apart, the figure being a little
slewed round with regard to the meridian." Mr Maunder discusses

them in the later Parsi writings had a planet for
special antagonist, for in the Magian system the
planets were creatures of Ahriman. Whether they
were really so in the pure Iranian Mazdeism may be
doubted, for they were named after the Yazatas—
Jupiter was Ormazd, Venus Anâhît, etc. It seems
at least possible that we have here a deep-lying
difference between the Aryan and the Magian strata
in Parsism. However this may be, we note that
more obviously Ahrimanian opponents are provided
in the meteors, which are called *Pairika*, "Peris" or
evil fairies. These Peris are conspicuous among the
creatures of the Evil Spirit, being regularly associated
with *Yâtus*, "sorcerers," who may be either demons
or men. It is suggestive that with this whole-hearted
abhorrence of sorcery in the forefront of the Maz-
dayasna, the very name of "magic" in the West
should be derived from the men who became priests
of that religion. The reason belongs to the develop-
ments described in Chap. VI. above.

The most important part of Yasht 8 is that which
describes the great fight between Tishtrya and his
opponent Apaosha, the Drought demon, a motive

some other stars, and makes some interesting suggestions as to the
possibility of using the legend for determining the date—a tempting
line, but beyond our limits here. The stars I have given are the
same as those for which Geiger decides (*Civilisation of the Eastern
Iranians*, I. 141), but he puts Satavaēsa in the West, wrongly inter-
preting the Pahlavi evidence (Bartholomae).

very suggestive of the Rigveda. We read how his
first appearance—his heliacal rising, or first emer-
gence from the sun's rays so as to shine before
sunrise—is eagerly awaited by "flocks and herds and
men." The myth itself occupies stanzas 13–34. Tishtrya appears at last, and for ten nights moves forward
in the form of a man in his prime : fifteen years is
the prime in the Avesta. Ten nights more he has
the form of a golden-horned bull, and then for ten
nights that of a white horse, in each case making
promises to men who will worship him—male children,
herds of oxen, troops of horses, according to his successive forms. In this last form he goes down to the
sea Vouru-kasha, the earth-encircling Ocean, in the
midst of which is the Shining Mount. But the demon
Apaosha rushes up to meet him as a black horse, and
(after a conflict of three days and three nights, if we
may follow the prose stanza 22) Tishtrya retires
baffled. At this crisis the prose interpolator signifi-
cantly steps in, to tell how Ahura Mazdâh offered
Tishtrya the sacrifice with his name invoked, the
neglect of which by men had produced this rout.
What original element in the story was ejected to
admit this characteristic accretion, the fellow to
which we met with in Yasht 5, we do not know.
That some power, probably enough Ahura, gave him
the strength of ten horses, ten camels, ten bulls,
ten mountains and ten rivers, is duly recorded

in verse ; and when after another prose interval
the poetic afflatus returns, the victory is achieved,
thanksgiving offered, and the rains descend.

Lack of space forbids comment on the miscellane-
ous praises that occupy the rest of the verse portion
of Yasht 8. Nor must we say much of the next
hymn. Drvâspa (or rather *Druâspa*, trisyllabic) is
a Yazata whose function according to her name is
to keep horses healthy. She is closely connected
with *Gĕuš-urvan* and *Gĕuš-tašan*, "Ox-soul" and
"Ox-fashioner," who were described above (pp. 87 f.,
91 f.): the Yasht accordingly may be compared with
the Gâthâ that deals with the subject (*Ys.* 29), to
point the contrast between Gâthâs and Yashts in
general. Practically the whole of Yasht 9 recurs in
the middle of the hymn addressed to Ashi Vanuhi
(*Yt.* 17). It is on lines familiar in the Yashts (see
p. 122), a list of Iranian heroes who sacrificed to the
Yazata and asked certain blessings, which are granted.
The list is identical in the two Yashts, in contents and
in order, and only the name of the divinity is changed :
the formula also which records the giving of the boon
is longer for Drvâspa than for Ashi. There are fuller
ritual interpolations in prose in the former Yasht.
Which was the original we cannot tell.

As might be expected, the Hymn to Mithra
(*Yt.* 10) is the most important of all the Yashts.
Enough has already been said (pp. 37, 55, and 88) of

the origin and character of this supremely important
Yazata. We have seen reason for regarding him
as originally the firmament, giver of light, which
primitive peoples may well have assigned to it
independently of sun and moon: we remember how
Light is anterior to "the lights" in Genesis. It is
as a Light-god that Franz Cumont regards Mithra.
To the fascinating pages of this great scholar we
refer those who would read how in parts of Iran
that were untouched by the Reformation the old
Aryan light-god more than regained his old prominence, and without associates like the Indian Varuṇa
and the Iranian (or Iranianised) Anâhita, took to
himself fresh features from Semitic religion and
began to dominate the West. The Mithra of Mithraism is not to be recognised in our Yasht as far as
we are concerned with it, even if Darmesteter is right
in tracing a dim feature of him in a prose addition.
What common elements exist descend from the
prehistoric Indo-Iranian period. The commanding
position of Mithra in that age is recalled in the
Yasht, it would seem, by a passage in verse, which
though fragmentary may be old, where Mithra and
Ahura are joined in a pair as "the two great im-
perishable, holy ones" (l. 145). We are familiar with
such association between Mazdâh and Asha or Vohu
Manah in the Gâthâs, and we have shown how entirely
consistent it is with the monotheism Zarathushtra

came to proclaim. But Mithra is another matter—
what concord hath Ahura with him?

The reader of the Yasht will find however that
the old Aryan divinity has assimilated himself very
successfully to his new environment. The utmost
is made of his function as Lord of Truth, the
preeminent Zarathushtrian virtue. The very first
verse-line of the hymn presents us with a splendid
declaration of the universal duty:—

> Spitama, break not the promise [*miθrem*]
> Made with sinner, made with faithful,
> Comrade in thy Law, for Mithra
> Stands for sinner, stands for faithful (*Yt.* 10²).

The hymn is mainly composed of instances to prove
that the invincible deity will crush the *miθradruj*—
where it does not matter whether we use a capital
initial or not, say "Mithra-deceiver" or "contract-
breaker"—and save him who is faithful to the genius
and what he represents. The desultory character of
the Yasht makes it difficult to summarise, and it will
suffice to pick out a few passages that are specially
noteworthy. The fifth canto may be quoted as fairly
typical: as before, we cite the prose, that the reader
may do his own higher criticism.

> Mithra, lord of spacious pastures [we worship][1]
> True of speech, and wise in council,
> With a thousand ears, well-shapen,
> With a myriad eyes, exalted,

[1] This may be a twelve-syllable line: see p. 18.

> From his worldwide watchtower gazing,
> Strong, unsleeping, ever watchful;

who is not deceived of any, whether lord of house, or lord of village, lord of town or lord of province. If the lord of a house, a village, a town or a province lies unto him,

> Then doth Mithra, fierce and angered,
> Crush the house and crush the village,
> Crush the town and crush the province,

and the lords of the houses, the villages, the towns, the provinces and the chief men of the provinces.

From this point Geldner notes the regular alternation of four-line and five-line stanzas (Vedic *Anuṣṭubh* and *Paṅkti* metres):—

> Thither Mithra, fierce and angered,
> Hies him forth where'er he findeth
> One that lies to him, and lying
> Cares not, for his heart is hardened.

> So the steeds of all those liars
> Fling their riders from the saddle:
> Though they run, one step they stir not,
> Though they ride, one pace they move not,
> Though they drive, one yard advance not.

> Backward lo! the spear is flying
> That the foe of Mithra hurleth,
> For the mass of magic mischief
> That the foe of Mithra worketh.

> Yea, though well he throws and truly,
> Though he reach his foeman's body,
> Yet to wound the strokes avail not,
> For the mass of magic mischief
> That the foe of Mithra worketh.

> Lo ! that spear the wind is warping
> That the foe of Mithra hurleth,
> For the mass of magic mischief
> That the foe of Mithra worketh (*Yt.* 10$^{17-21}$).

Darmesteter explains this recurring phrase by noting
that "the sacramental words of the contract, by
their not being kept, turn to evil spells against
the contract-breaker." Our next quotation has an
interesting resemblance to a gem of European poetry,
that lovely passage in the *Odyssey* which Lucretius
even bettered in the borrowing, and our own great
poet wove into his picture of the "island valley of
Avilion." It is a curious coincidence that just as
Homer idealises Olympus, till commentators dispute
whether his "seat of the gods" is on earth at all,
even so the Persian holy mountain Hara Berezaiti
or Alburz ("High Mountain") is ambiguously the
dominating feature of an earthly landscape or a
mythic peak wholly appropriated to the divine. But
let us give the lines as well as we can, for here at last
the translator feels a shrinking as he lays his hand
on poetry :—

> For him Mazdāh the Creator
> Reared a palace on the Mountain,
> Alburz, with its hills encircled,
> Glorious, where nor night nor darkness
> Climbs, nor blows the chill, the searching
> Wind, nor sickness comes death-dealing,
> Nor the devil-born pollution ;
> Nor upon that Mighty Mountain
> Are the dark clouds seen ascending (*Yt.* 10^{50}).

It is characteristic that the orthodox and con-
scientious interpolator feels himself bound to add in
prose, helped out with an irrelevant couplet from an
earlier canto, that the Amesha Spentas made the
palace of Mithra, "in one accord with the Sun."
One more extract claims a place.

> He from whom true Glory fleeth,
> From the straightest path forwandered,
> In his inmost heart hath sorrow.
> Thus he thinketh, that Inglorious,
> "Blind is Mithra: all the ill deeds,
> All the lying words, he sees not."
> But, for me, I think within me,
> "Surely nowhere under heaven
> Is a worldly man who thinketh
> Evil thoughts to match the good thoughts
> Of the spiritual Mithra" (Yt. $10^{105t.}$).

And so for words and deeds, *mutatis mutandis*.   The
parallels in the Psalms are obvious.   *Duš-χ^{v}arenå*,
"one who has evil glory," suggests the Hebrew name
Ichabod, but only superficially.   "Glory" is a technical word, as we shall see when we come to Yasht
19; and it should be remembered in connexion with
the present passage that its possession depends abso-
lutely on truthfulness.

One or two snatches of verse are not adequate
warrant for our staying on the eleventh Yasht,
addressed to Sraosha.   For the same reason we shall
be content with naming the twelfth (to Rashnu), the
sixteenth (to Chista, or the creed of Zarathushtra—an

obviously late composition, wholly in prose), and the
eighteenth, a short prose piece (except for one stanza),
which occupies itself with the same subject as the one
next to it. Only two really important hymns are left.
The thirteenth, to the Fravashis, is the longest of all,
but in only about half of its stanzas does it show
even single lines of verse. There is an interesting
problem in it which affects its date. In l. [16] we read
how the Fravashis cause a man to be born who is
a master in assemblies and skilled in sacred lore, so
that he "comes away from debate" a victor over
"Gaotema." Now Gotama, which answers exactly
to this, is a Vedic proper name, and Bartholomae
is satisfied with recognising an otherwise unknown
unbeliever. Geldner (in 1877) took it as a common
noun. But the temptation to see here Gautama the
Buddha is extremely strong. Darmesteter says that
Buddhism had established a footing in Western Iran
as early as the second century B.C. Professor Cowell
used to point out that *praçna*, the cognate of the
word rendered "debate" just now, was a prominent
word in Buddhism. On the same side is a concise
and telling argument in Prof. Jackson's *Zoroaster*,
pp. 177 f. Accepting this view, first suggested by
Haug, we are, in Darmesteter's opinion, brought
down to the age of the Arsacid dynasty; but there
hardly seems adequate reason for rejecting the possibility that isolated missionaries of Buddhism might

have been found in Iran many generations earlier, and Prof. Jackson gives a good argument for this earlier date drawn from the Yasht itself. One might even hazard the suggestion that the mistake by which the name of Gautama is transferred to a man who preached Gautama's gospel, may be due to the very fact that the preaching was thus isolated, that Buddhism was still almost unknown.

Much might be written here on the subject of the Fravashis, by far the most interesting of the conceptions which appear (or more probably reappear) in the age immediately following Zarathushtra. The etymological meaning of the name is wisely left as unknown in Bartholomae's Lexicon. It is often given as "confession" or "belief," for which might be pleaded the curious coincidence that in the Gâthâs the word *daēnā* combines two senses (or two different words), the (Zarathushtrian) Law and the Ego of a man, an idea not far away from that of the Fravashi. But everything else in the picture of these beings seems to make against this interpretation. Very tentatively we would suggest another account, coming directly from one of the Fravashis' functions. There is an Avestan root *var*, "to impregnate," and *fravaši* might mean "birth-promotion." This takes us back to one of the most primitive functions of ancestor-spirits, who in sundry savage tribes are believed to be responsible for the pregnancy of women. (Cf.

J. G. Frazer, *Totemism and Exogamy*, I. 191, II. 508, *Adonis, Attis and Osiris*, pp. 76 ff.) Whether our guess is right or wrong, there is no question as to the prominence of this function of the Fravashis in the Yasht, nor any doubt that it is a function entirely appropriate to ancestor-spirits. No less appropriate, according to universal folklore, is their puissance in war, which is very conspicuous in the Yasht. Less easy to account for is their intimate connexion with the Waters. Dr Frazer notes for me the fact that in ancient Greece a good many people claimed to be descended from rivers, referring me to his *Pausanias*, I. p. lix; but it does not seem to be a very prominent function of the Manes to preside over waters. Perhaps it is only derived from their connexion with childbirth, with which water-spirits had a great deal to do in Avestan lore: compare especially Yasht 5. There is also a connexion with the stars, rather doubtfully suggested in this Yasht, and proclaimed in a Pahlavi treatise which lies somewhat aside from the full stream of Parsi orthodoxy. This obviously suits their identification with spirits of the dead. The identification is clearly Aryan. The Pitáras or "Fathers" of the Vedic system have many features in common with them. The last-mentioned, their not very strongly developed stellar character, recalls the fact that in the Veda the Fathers "are said to have adorned the sky with stars and placed darkness in the night and light in the day" (Macdonell, *Vedic Mythology*, p. 171). Similarly (*Yt.* 13[57 f.]) the Fravashis "showed their paths to the sun, the moon, the sun and the endless lights." It must be allowed that though they thus "preserve the stars from wrong," this falls short of identification with stars: probably the Magian element in the theology of the Fravashis was mainly responsible for the equation which produces the inference of the Magi in the second chapter of our first Gospel. Deeply rooted in the ritual of Parsism, and clearly indicated in the rather broken verse of ll. [49-52], is the annual All Souls' feast in honour of the Fravashis. Like the Athenians and the Romans, the Parsis kept it at the end of the year, just before the opening of spring, when the Fravashis were invited to abide with their living friends; and after the five intercalary days were over and the New Year dawned, they departed leaving a blessing. The rite is worldwide—see J. G. Frazer's *Adonis, Attis and Osiris*, pp. 301—320. One further trait, conspicuous in a recurrent formula of this Yasht, "the Fravashis of the righteous," gets its explanation from the ancestral character of these spirits. They are the *Manes*, "the good folk"; and when their original features were lost they were bound to be attached, as objects of worship, to the righteous alone. (See Söderblom, *Les Fravashis*, p. 66.)

But this is not all. In l. [17], a verse passage and

therefore presumably original, we read that the most
powerful Fravashis were those of the men of the
primitive law (cf. above, p. 130) or the still unborn
Saoshyants who will restore the world. Next to
these, "the Fravashis of the living righteous are
more powerful than those of the dead." They are
therefore not only ancestor spirits. The later Parsi
books tell us that the Fravashi is a part of a good
man's identity, living in heaven and reuniting with
the soul at death. It is not exactly a guardian angel,
for it shares in the development or deterioration of
the rest of the man. It is in fact derived from the
well-known primitive concept of the External Soul,
described at length by Dr Frazer (*Golden Bough*[2],
III. 351 ff.). It seems reasonable to attribute this
totally distinct element to the non-Aryan Magi[1], who
will thus have laid hold of the old Aryan doctrine
and imported their own ideas before the Yasht
was composed, or the ideas on which it was based
developed. The prose parts of the Yashts are
full of names of heroes male and female, Aryan
and Turanian, born and unborn, whose fravashis
are adored. These must not detain us. We will
only stay now to cite one passage whereby the

---

[1] On this reference may be made to the writer's papers, "It is
His Angel" (*Journ. of Theol. Studies*, 1902, pp. 514 ff.) and "Syn-
cretism in Religion, as illustrated in the History of Parsism" (Oxford
Congress of the History of Religions, esp. II. 99 f.).

quality of the Yasht in its original kernel may be
gauged.

> By their brightness and their glory,
> Zarathushtra, I stay from ruin
> Yonder heaven, sublime and shining,
> That the whole earth doth encompass ;
> Like a palace spirit-fashioned,
> Stablished, far withdrawn its limit,
> With the form of glowing metal,
> Lightens it the world's three regions.
> With that heaven, as with a garment
> Star-embroidered, spirit-woven,
> Mazdâh clothes him and his angels,
> Mithra, Rashnu, Aramaiti ;
> Nor on any side beginning
> Nor an end thereof appeareth (*Yt.* 13²ᵗ·).

The fourteenth Yasht is a medley, of no special
interest. It is addressed to Verethraghna, the genius
of Victory, whose successive avatars in various animal
and human forms are the subject of its longest section.
We have already (pp. 39 f.) remarked on the original
character of Verethraghna as an Aryan divinity,
already unintelligible in name when the Indian tribes
migrated. There is much in this Yasht that is sheer
magic : spells and talismans for success in battle
belong to the most primitive of savages, and relics
of savagery survive most naturally in connexion with
war. There is some vigour in the description of the
vāreɣna bird, the seventh avatar of the Genius ; but
we have no space to quote it (*Yt.* 14²⁰ ᶠ·). Still less

are we disposed to linger over the "late hackwork,"
as Bartholomae calls it, of the fifteenth Yasht, dedicated to Vayu, the atmosphere.   We pass on accordingly to the seventeenth, though here also for no
lengthy survey. *Aši Vaṅuhi*, "good reward," is a
personification of Gâthic antiquity: good and bad
rewards alike appear in the ancient hymns, and
in *Ys.* 31⁴ Ashi is named without epithet in close
connexion with Aramaiti.   In the Later Avesta she
becomes the genius of the blessings assigned to piety.
Her etymological association with Asha must not be
depended on: the names have only the root in common, and the conceptions do not touch. In the Yasht
Ashi is rather like the Latin Fortuna.   She gives all
manner of wealth and prosperity to a series of the
faithful who court her (see above on *Yt.* 9); and in
particular she blesses marriage.   Her affection for
Zarathushtra is expressed in the only passage that
tempts us in any way to quote, illustrating as it does
the contrast with the wholly human Prophet of the
Gâthâs.

> Thus she spake then, the Good Ashi,
> She the lofty one, "Come nearer,
> True and holy Zarathushtra,
> Lean thee here against my chariot."
> Nearer to her came Spitâma,
> On her car leaned Zarathushtra.
> From above she then caressed him
> With the left arm and the right arm,
> With the right arm and the left arm;

> Thus she then with words addressed him :
> "Beauteous art thou, Zarathushtra,
> Shapely art thou, O Spitâma ;
> Fair of limb and long i' th' arm thou.
> Glory to thy body is given,
> To thy soul long bliss in heaven,
> Sure as that I thus have spoken " (*Yt.* 17²¹ᵗ·).

These lovely verses of ours are without unseemly
pride guaranteed equal to the original, which, however, in the fourth line from the end has "with
beautiful calves"—*quod versu dicere non est*! It
may be added that long arms were a beauty: Artaxerxes Longimanus (*Dirazdast*) might seem to own
a nickname, rather like our own King Longshanks,
but the resemblance is misleading.

Practically last among the Yashts proper comes
the nineteenth, the most original of all, as Geldner
calls it. It is devoted to the "Glory" ($\chi^v arenah$—
see above, p. 43), and the heroes who attained it,
from Ahura Mazdâh down to Saoshyant. As Darmesteter observes, the Yasht "would serve as a short
history of the Iranian monarchy, an abridged Shâh
Nâmeh." It begins with the ninth stanza of the
hymn as given in our MSS., being very irrelevantly
tacked on to a prose enumeration of mountains.
Then we open with stanzas which recur thrice in
the later parts of the Yasht, with of course a variation
each time as a new recipient of the Glory is described.
Prose tells us that the Powerful Kingly Glory is

worshipped, which belongs to Ahura (the Ameshas, the
Yazatas, the Saoshyants). Then, with various attach-
ments, come these verses, which obviously might as
well have been composed for any other Yasht.

> That the world they may establish,
> Ne'er henceforth to age or perish,
> Ne'er corrupting, ne'er decaying,
> Ever living, ever growing,
> Master of itself......;
> When, the dead to new life rising,
> He[1] the Living, Unimperilled,
> Cometh, and the world's desiring
> Shall be sated with renewal.
> Then, to Asha's Law obedient,
> Shall creation aye be deathless,
> And the Lie be thither driven
> Whence she came......　　(*Yt.* 19[11f.]).

" The rest was prose," to cite the suggestive colophon
from one of Milton's early poems; and as our print-
ing indicates, the fragment has suffered metrically in
transmission.　　But it is worth citing to compare with
Gâthic eschatology.　　As will be seen when we come
to the beautiful " Yasht 22," the doctrine of the Last
Things is the side of Parsism that has been least
marred in the interval between Zarathushtra and the
Sassanian revival.　　A further comparison with the
Gâthâs may be suggested by the passage about Yima

---

[1] i.e. Saoshyant.

(see pp. 42 ff.). (The gaps again roughly indicate flaws
in the metre.)

> From the Devils plundered Yima
> Riches, welfare, flocks and fatness,
> Peace and honour bare he from them.
> By his sovranty abounded
> Ever food and drink unfailing.
> Flocks and men were all undying,
> Waters, plants, no fell drought touched them;
> Neither cold nor hot wind blowing,
> Neither eld nor death, nor envy
> Devil-born were............,
> Ere he first to lies and untruth
> Bent his thought and tongue......
> Then before all eyes the Glory
> Bird-like fled away from Yima.
> When he saw the Glory vanish,
> Yima Khshaēta, noble shepherd,
> Rushed he round distraught, and smitten
> By his foes on earth he laid him (*Yt.* 19³²ᶠᶠ.).

It will be seen by this time that the "Glory" is
a mythical talisman which belonged essentially to
the royal house of Iran, though two-thirds of it
vanished with Yima's sin. It is noteworthy that the
succession comes down no further than Víshtâspa,
passing on immediately to Saoshyant, who belongs
to eschatology alone. The opportunity of bringing
in Cyrus and Darius was not taken. It may well be
that the Yasht—and consequently perhaps much else
in the Yashts—was composed either before their day

or in another part of Iran: if the latter, the rulers of
that district equally missed celebration. Of course
we know too little about the conditions to attach
great weight to such argument. We may note in
passing that the Glory was prominent enough in
Western Iran in the Achaemenid period: proper
names like Tissaphernes and Intaphernes contain its
Old Persian equivalent (*farna*ʰ).

There is one passage in this Yasht which we may
refer to for the sake of the interesting literary parallel
drawn by Darmesteter. The famous Iranian hero
Keresâspa seized the Glory when it departed the
third time from Yima, and among other monsters he
killed Snâvidhaka, whose boast was:—

> Child I am as yet—if ever
> With the years I come to full age,
> I will make the earth a whirling
> Wheel, and of the heaven my chariot.
> I will drag blest Spenta Mainyu
> Down from shining House of Singing;
> I will speed fell Angra Mainyu
> Up from dreary Home of Evil.
> They shall draw for me my chariot,
> Those twain Spirits, Blest and Evil—
> If he do not first assail me,
> He, brave-hearted Keresâspa (*Yt.* 19⁴³ᶠ·)—

which of course, according to the prose, he promptly
did. Darmesteter compares Otus and Ephialtes in

the *Odyssey*, who were nine fathoms high at nine
years, and threatened the Immortals:—

Aye and the deed had they done, had they reached but the
    noontide of life;
But Zeus' and Leto's son destroyed them in that first strife,
Or ever, their temples beneath, bloomed blossom of young down
    fair,
Or on chin and on cheek as a wreath fell the shadow of clustering
    hair (*Od.* XI. 314 ff. Way's translation).

We have by no means exhausted the interest of
this Yasht, but we have outstripped our space, and
other things to be named raise problems too difficult
for us here. There is no more verse in the Yashts,
as printed in Geldner's great critical edition. For the
only remaining poems of the kind we turn to the later
parts of the Yasna, where hymns are found to Haoma
(*Ys.* 9—11) and to Sraosha (*Ys.* 57). These Yazatas
are among the very highest in the pre-Zarathushtrian
and the Reformed periods respectively. Haoma, the
Indian Soma, was an intoxicating drink, prepared by
crushing the stalk of a plant very doubtfully identified.
In the Veda it is of pre-eminent importance, but Zarathushtra (as might have been expected) preserved a
severe silence about it, if indeed he did not expressly
denounce so demoralising an element in the national
religion. So at least Bartholomae reads *Ys.* 32[14]—
compare what was said on this Gâthâ above, p. 97,
also p. 110. When this Bacchic divinity emerged from

his eclipse, he seems to have been to some extent sobered into a reformed character: we have no particular evidence of alcohol, and Haoma appears to have become mostly magical or mystical. One interesting old folklore story may be quoted in Prof. L. H. Mills's words: it is an exploit of Keresâspa.

> He who smote the horny dragon swallowing men and swallowing horses, poisonous, and green of colour, over which, as thick as thumbs are, greenish poison flowed aside; on whose back once Keresâspa cooked his meat in iron caldron at the noonday meal; and the deadly, scorched, upstarted, and springing off, dashed out the water as it boiled. Headlong fled affrighted manly-minded Keresâspa (*Ys.* 9¹¹—see *S. B. E.* XXXI. 234).

(The places where the rhythm fails in Dr Mills's version do not quite answer to the weak spots in the original metric: we print it as prose, as he does.) There is an amusing comment by the Pahlavi translator upon the hero's "affrighted" flight. "His manly-mindedness was this, that he kept his wits on the occasion." We need not be careful to excuse Keresâspa too elaborately for his fright under circumstances that were obviously trying. The story occurs in practically the same form in *Yt.* 19⁴⁰, where Darmesteter's version (*S. B. E.* XXIII. 295) may be compared. Another touch of folklore may be cited from this hymn, the prayer addressed to Haoma:—

> First may we be ware of robber,
> First of wolf and first of bandit:
> Let them not of us be first ware,
> Let us of them all be first ware (*Ys.* 9²¹).

We compare at once Virgil's familiar "lupi Moerim videre priores."

Nor may we overlook the promise that follows :—

> They that long sit searching scriptures,
> Haoma grants them grace and knowledge ($Y_s.$ 9^{22}).

The *Nasks* or "scriptures" here mentioned mean essentially no doubt the Gâthâs, for if the word means the Avesta as a whole—which was in Sassanian times divided into 21 Nasks—we must put this verse fragment too late.

The hymn to Sraosha does not present anything special to dwell on, and we have now come very nearly to the end of the poetry of the Avesta. There are plenty of scraps of verse scattered up and down the prose portions of the Parsi scriptures; but in a little book which cannot be exhaustive we are justified in passing them by. Two compositions alone we can find space for. The second fargard (chapter) of the Vendîdâd is almost isolated in the Leviticus of Parsism as containing a fairly long piece of continuous verse, and subject-matter of real interest. It is the story of Yima (see pp. 41 ff.), of whom Ahura Mazdâh tells Zarathushtra that he was the first mortal before him to receive the revelation of Ahura.

> Spake I to him, Zarathushtra,
> I that am the Lord of Wisdom,
> "Keeper be thou, beauteous Yima,
> Bearer of my Revelation."

> But the beauteous Yima answered,
> "Not for this was I appointed,
> Nor was taught, to be the keeper,
> Bearer of the Revelation."
> Spake I to him, Zarathushtra,
> I that am the Lord of Wisdom,
> "If thou wilt not be the keeper,
> Bearer of my Revelation,
> Prosper thou my good Creation,
> Increase thou my good Creation,
> Be thou Guardian, Overseer,
> Watcher over my Creation" (*Vend.* 2^{2-4}).

Yima agrees, but the text becomes corrupt for a stanza or two. The result is that for three hundred years

> Then the earth became abounding,
> Full of flocks and full of cattle,
> Full of men, of birds, dogs likewise,
> Full of fires all bright and blazing,
> Nor did men, flocks, herds of cattle,
> Longer find them places on it
>   (*Vend.* 2^8—tr. A. V. W. Jackson).

In response to the Creator's warning Yima has his remedy for overcrowding, which lasts another three centuries, to be finally repeated for a third period. Death and disease being unknown, this successive enlargement of the earth by increments of one-third each time—so the prose says—saves the situation up to the end of Yima's reign: for this end see above, p. 43. Here is his expedient:—

> He the earth with golden arrow
> Clave, and bored her with his poniard,
> Saying "Holy Aramaiti,
> Stretch thee widely, cleave asunder" (*Vend.* 2^{10}).

The identification of Aramaiti and the Earth will be noted. The second half of this fargard is peculiarly interesting to us, but is in prose, a rare exception to the rule that the verse parts monopolise the interest. It tells of the Vara, the refuge Yima built on Ahura's suggestion to shelter mankind and animals from a terrible winter. The picture strongly tempts us to recognise the influence of the Babylonian Flood-story: if so, it is very noteworthy that the hall-mark of lateness, prose, should be stamped upon this almost solitary specimen of borrowed matter. The prose warns us off here, or we should have liked to observe that the Vara recalls Revelation more even than Genesis—it is a city, built foursquare, with a river through it, as one of the only two scraps of verse tells us :—

> Make a river there of water,
> In a mile-long channel lead it ;
> There establish grassy meadows,
> There establish pleasant mansions (*Vend.* 2^{26}).

We take leave of the Vendîdâd with two typical contrasted extracts. One is the benediction upon the ritualist :—

> "Unto thee of cattle plenty,
> Unto thee be wealth of children,
> Unto thee be active spirit,
> Active soul attend upon thee!
> Live with joyful-minded being
> All the nights that here thou livest!"
>   Such is Âtar's blessing on him,
> Whoso bringeth to him fuel,
> Dried, prepared for clear bright burning,
> Cleansed with rite of holy service (*Vend.* 18²⁷).

The prose that precedes tells us that of two bed-fellows who hear the cock crowing, the one who gets up first shall first enter Paradise; and the one who feeds the fire (Âtar) will receive the above blessing. This ritual, as any housewife will cheerfully acknowledge, is of an eminently practical character—which cannot be said of all rituals. In the same fargard we have an antithesis which gives the deeper side of the religion, setting against one another the false Âthravan (fire-priest) and the true.

> "Him shalt call by priestly title,"
> So he spake, the Lord of Wisdom,
> "O thou holy Zarathushtra,
> Who throughout the time of darkness
> Still enquires of holy Wisdom.
>   *   *   *
> Ask of me, the great Creator,
> Most beneficent of beings,
> That for thee there may be blessing,
> That thyself may be the happier,
> If thou make enquiry of me" (*Vend.* 18⁷ᶠ).

We close with a freer description of a true poem, which paradoxically enough comes to us mainly in prose. Westergaard included it in his Avesta as Yasht 22, for which Geldner corrects him. We could have easily forgiven the veteran Professor for making the same mistake, and so finding room in his monumental work for a critical edition of this beautiful piece. It is a picture of the passage of the soul after death. We can hardly say how old its material is. On the one side it touches the Gâthâs, with which it is truly one in spirit; on the other it comes near to the Pahlavi Vision of Ardâ Vîrâf, the Parsi analogue of the "Apocalypse of Peter" and similar predecessors of Dante's *Divine Comedy*. Perhaps as it is the thoughts more than the words that can be described as poetry, we may represent it best in a free modern substitute, in which we may try to gather together the eschatology of Parsism from first to last. For such a purpose we must ask to be excused presenting the obverse of the medal: whoever will may go through our halting verses and by substituting devils for angels, hideous hags for lovely maidens, and so forth, gain an accurate idea of the mechanically balanced fate which the seer prepared for the wicked. The details will mostly be clear from explanations given up and down this little book: it is intended that the index should enable readers to find them.

AD ASTRA.

Glory to thee, O Mazdâh! Lo, I turn
From dazzling visions of Thy home of light,
And find me weary in the strife again,
To battle with the watchful fiends that line
Man's path to Heaven. Yet in the sacred Fire
I pray Thee let my waking thoughts recall
Sights that can soothe and strengthen.
                              I beheld,
And lo, from out the eternal House of Song,
One came and answered my unspoken prayer:—
"How came I hither? Thou must tell the tale
Of what I was, a mortal, for the years
Of bliss have swept the memory away.
It may be the fell demons of disease
Vanquished my body, while the Death-fiend nigh
Waited the hour to swoop upon her prey.
What recked I? I was free.
                        Three days I watched
Hard by the spot whence weeping friends had borne
The demon-haunted frame that once was mine.
New light had dawned on all the earthly scenes
Where once I seemed to struggle all alone
Against the Lie; for myriad angel forms
Thronged o'er the foughten field, and silently
Strengthened the weary warrior with their aid.
And joy whose like the world had never known
Bade me forget the tears that death had drawn
And death should dry.
                    Four glorious Dawns had risen,
And with the wakening loveliness of day
Came breezes whispering from the southern sky,
Laden with fragrant sweetness. I beheld,

And floating lightly on the enamoured winds
A Presence sped and hovered over me,
A maiden, roseate as the blush of morn,
Stately and pure as heaven, and on her face
The freshness of a bloom untouched of Time.
Amazed I cried, 'Who art thou, Maiden fair,
Fairer than aught on earth these eyes have seen?'
And she in answer spake, 'I am Thyself,
Thy thoughts, thy words, thy actions, glorified
By every conquest over base desire,
By every offering of a holy prayer
To the Wise Lord in Heaven, every deed
Of kindly help done to the good and pure.
By these I come thus lovely, come to guide
Thy steps to the dread Bridge where waits for thee
The Prophet, charged with judgement.'
                                        On the winds
A little space we flew, yet spanned therein
Ten times the gulf that severs sun and star,
On to the South, where like a buried noon
Glimmered a growing glory—onward still,
Till heavens burning with ethereal light
Revealed the House of Song. High-towered it stood,
With flashing diamonds walled, suspense in air;
And, far beneath, a chasm fathomless
To keenest vision, whence a muffled wail
Strained through the solid darkness and betrayed
Fell Angra Mainyu's realm. Long time I gazed
Dazzled at Heaven, or blinded upon Hell;
Till o'er the abyss I saw a thin bright line
Stretched up to that fair portal, and I knew
The Bridge of Judgement. Lo, an angel dread
Sat there beside, and in his hand the scales
To weigh the good and evil. At his bar

I stood, yet feared not, while good angels pled
And demons fierce accused me, till the scale
Sank with the load of everlasting joy.
So with my Angel forth I sped and passed
The Bridge of Judgement, passed the Heavens Three,
Good Thought, Good Word, Good Action, and beyond
Soared to the place of Everlasting Light,
Ahura Mazdâh's boundless House of Song.
A Saint's voice hailed me, "How hast hither come,
From carnal world to spiritual, from the realm
Of death to life, to bliss that cannot die ?
And from the Throne came answer, 'Question not
Him that hath trod the dread and unknown path
Which parts the body and the soul for aye.'"

O Thou Wise Lord, who when Thy world was young
  Didst pierce the grim night of the eastern sky
  With gladsome rays of truth and purity,
Forgive the error of this venturous song
That strives to hymn Thy bounty. May my tongue
  Tell of Thy Seer, and how against the Lie
  Pure thoughts, pure words, pure actions' victory
Rang from his herald trumpet loud and long:—
So from the blaze wherein Thy glories dwell
  Once more athwart the sunless gloom a Star
  Shall flash its guiding message, and from far
The Sage of Iran answer to the spell,
  And speed with trophies of a faith long dim
  To find his Lord and bow the knee to Him.

BIBLIOGRAPHY

A few of the most necessary books for study are mentioned here. Generally speaking, those which are named in the text are not repeated.

A. TEXT, GRAMMAR AND LEXICON

Geldner. Avesta, the Sacred Books of the Parsis. Stuttgart, 1886—1895. Also published in German. The only obtainable text, superseding all others.

Jackson, A. V. W. An Avesta Grammar. Part I (all published). Stuttgart, 1892. The most convenient Grammar, but difficult to get.

—— Avesta Reader: First Series. Easier Texts, Notes and Vocabulary. Stuttgart, 1893.

Bartholomae, C. Vorgeschichte der iranischen Sprachen; also Awestasprache und Altpersisch. In vol. I. of Geiger and Kuhn's Grundriss der iranischen Philologie. Strassburg, 1896—1904. Very elaborate and full.

—— Handbuch der Zendsprache. A Grammar, with chrestomathy and vocabulary. Leipzig, 1883.

—— Altiranisches Wörterbuch. Strassburg, 1905. An indispensable book.

Justi, F. Handbuch der Zendsprache. Leipzig, 1864. For forty years our only Avestan dictionary. Named here because in its Chrestomathie it has a text of "Yasht 22," which Geldner does not include.

B. Translations

Darmesteter and Mills. The Zend-Avesta. In Sacred Books of the East, 3 vols. Vol. I. (ed.[2]) contains Darmesteter's theory as to the date of the Avesta, and translation of the Vendîdâd; vol. II. translates the Yashts; vol. III. (by Prof. Mills) the Gâthâs and later Yasna.

Mills, L. H. The Hymns of Zoroaster, Bombay, 1909. This little book (to be obtained from the Cooper Publishing Company, Ilford, London) contains Dr Mills's "free" translations of the Gâthâs without commentary. As metre they mainly illustrate the impossibility of rendering the Gâthâs into anything but prose; but the version must be studied for the reason given under the next-cited work.

—— The Five Zoroastrian Gâthâs. Leipzig, 1894. This encyclopaedic work is indispensable for the student of the original, because of the traditional material it contains.

Bartholomae, C. Die Gatha's des Awesta. Zarathushtra's Verspredigten, übersetzt von C. B. Strassburg, 1905. A beautiful little book, the latest and most trustworthy version. There is perhaps somewhat too much originality in the lexicographer's work, which is very often found differing widely from the other authorities, see above, p. 82 f.

Wolff, F. Avesta. A German translation based on Bartholomae's Lexicon. The Gâthâs are omitted. Strassburg, 1910.

Casartelli, L. C. Leaves from my Eastern Garden. Market Weighton, 1908. A little collection of verse renderings, mostly from the Avesta : these include $Yt.$ 19^{30-38}, 8^{20-33}, $Vend.$ 19 (and its Pahlavi), and three hymns of the Gâthâs. There is also a free adaptation of "$Yt.$ 22" and its kindred material, planned in much the same way as that given above, but closer to the Avestan texts.

Cooper, Nasarvanji M. The Imitation of Zoroaster. Quotations from Zoroastrian Literature. Ilford, London, 1910. A convenient little collection of maxims from early and later Parsi writings.

C. LITERATURE AND RELIGION OF THE AVESTA

Geldner. Awestalitteratur. In the Grundriss (see above), vol. II. A concise and masterly sketch. The same volume contains authoritative accounts of all branches of Iranian literature to modern times, also of the history and civilisations of Iran.

—— Articles "Persia" (pp. 246f.), "Zend-Avesta" and "Zoroaster" in Encyclopaedia Britannica, ed. [11].

Jackson, A. V. W. Die iranische Religion. In the same volume of the Grundriss. This is the fullest and best account we have.

—— Zoroaster. New York, 1899. An indispensable monograph, giving all the material there is for the history of Zoroaster, and the legends that have grown up round his name. The dissertations on his date and the sphere of his work are peculiarly valuable.

Lehmann, E. Die Perser, in Chantepie de la Saussaye's Religionsgeschichte, II. 162—233. Tübingen, 1905. An admirable sketch.

Tiele, C. P. Geschichte der Religion im Altertum, vol. II. Gotha, 1903. This volume (translated from Dutch) is entirely devoted to Parsism.

Carnoy, A. Religion of the Avesta. London (Catholic Truth Society). An excellent summary in a penny pamphlet, by a Louvain Professor.

Geiger, A. Civilisation of the Eastern Iranians in Ancient Times. London, 1885. An excellent and readable description, in two volumes, translated by the Parsi Dastur Peshotan Sanjānā.

Söderblom, N. La Vie Future d'après de Mazdéisme. Paris, 1901. A very full monograph on Avestan and post-Avestan eschatology.

Cumont, F. Textes et Monuments figurés relatifs aux Mystères de Mithra. Brussels, 1899. The great authority on Mithraism.

INDEXES

(1) PASSAGES OF THE AVESTA

(2) GENERAL

(Avestan or other Iranian words in italics)

www.ingramcontent.com/pod-product-compliance
Ingram Content Group UK Ltd.
Pitfield, Milton Keynes, MK11 3LW, UK
UKHW042144280225
455719UK00001B/80